FAMOUS REGIMENTS

The South Wales Borderers

FAMOUS REGIMENTS

EDITED BY

LT.-GENERAL SIR BRIAN HORROCKS

The South Wales Borderers

(The 24th Regiment of Foot)

BY

JACK ADAMS

HAMISH HAMILTON
LONDON

INTRODUCTION TO THE SERIES

by

LT.-GENERAL SIR BRIAN HORROCKS

IT IS ALWAYS sad when old friends depart. In the last few years many famous old regiments have disappeared, merged into larger formations.

I suppose this is inevitable; strategy and tactics are always changing, forcing the structure of the Army to change too. But the memories of the past still linger in minds now trained to great technical proficiency and surrounded by sophisticated equipment. Nevertheless the disappearance of these well-known names as separate units marks the end of a military epoch; but we must never forget that, throughout the years, each of these regiments has carved for itself a special niche in British History. The qualities of the British character, both good and bad, which helped England to her important position in the world can be seen at work in the regiments of the old Army. To see why these regiments succeeded under Marlborough and Wellington yet failed in the American War of Independence should help us in assessing the past.

Though many Battle Honours were won during historic campaigns, the greatest contribution which our Regiments have made to the British Empire is rarely mentioned: this has surely been the protection they have afforded to those indomitable British merchants, who in search of fresh markets spread our influence all over the world. For some of these this involved spending many years in stinking garrisons overseas where their casualties from disease were often far greater than those suffered on active service.

The main strength of our military system has always lain in the fact that regimental roots were planted deep into the British countryside in the shape of the Territorial Army, whose battalions are also subject to the cold winds of change. This ensured the closest possible link between civilian and military worlds, and built up a unique County and family *esprit de corps* which exists in no other Army in the world. A Cockney regiment, a West Country regiment and a Highland regiment differed from each other greatly, though they fought side by side in scores of battles. In spite of miserable conditions and savage discipline, a man often felt he belonged within the regiment—he shared the background and the hopes of his fellows. That was a great comfort for a soldier. Many times, at Old Comrades' gatherings, some old soldier has come up to me and said, referring to one of the World Wars, 'They were good times, sir, weren't they?'

They were not good times at all. They were horrible times; but what these men remember and now miss was the comradeship and *esprit de corps* of the old regular regiments. These regiments, which bound men together and helped them through the pain and fear of war, deserve to be recalled.

Regimental histories are usually terribly dull, as the authors are forced to record the smallest operation and include as many names as possible. In this series we have something new. Freed from the tyranny of minute detail, the authors have sought to capture that subtle quarry, the regimental spirit. The history of each regiment is a story of a type of British life now fading away. These stories illuminate the past, and should help us to think more clearly about the military future.

THE SOUTH WALES BORDERERS

A Special Introduction by

LT.-GENERAL SIR BRIAN HORROCKS

Over the years, the name of the South Wales Borderers has become almost synonymous with Rorke's Drift, where on the 22nd January 1879 their B Company beat off the savage attack of 3,000 Zulus flushed with success after recent victories over the British, and thus saved the lives of many white settlers in Natal. It was a typically staunch Welsh performance and was recognized as such by the award of no less than seven V.C.s to the Regiment. The 2nd Battalion had already won five similar awards for their gallantry when rowing ashore in the face of stiff resistance during their policing of the Andaman islands in 1865.

Without detracting in the least from the toughness and heroism displayed during both these operations, I am sure the Regiment themselves would be the first to admit that winning the V.C. has become progressively more difficult over the years. During the last war between 1939–45 I never succeeded once in obtaining this very rare decoration for anyone under my command in spite of several recommendations for deeds of the utmost gallantry. Nevertheless since they were first formed as the 24th Foot some 270 years ago the South Wales Borderers have earned for themselves the reputation of being one of the best fighting units in the British Army.

It is an established fact that all British Infantry Regiments develop their own particular family feeling which is obviously very dependent on their upbringing. The 24th Foot were lucky. Some thirteen years after formation they came under the influence of the greatest soldier this country has ever produced, the Duke of Marlborough, who became their colonel. Under his command they took part in all his famous battles during the War of the Spanish Succession—Blenheim, Ramillies, Oudenarde, Malplaquet and so on—when he soundly defeated the French Armies which had hitherto dominated Europe. But to my mind more important still than the Duke's strategical and tactical ability was the fact that he was the first Senior Commander who really cared about the welfare of the troops under his command. And it is this Marlborough tradition, continuing over the years and passed on from one colonel to the next, which has created that great family spirit which has always been such a marked feature of this regiment. No wonder that inspecting officers have been able to report 'the men are cheerful and speak up well'—always the sign of an efficient happy unit. It was this background which stood them in good stead during the holocaust of the 1914–18 War. On the 3rd December 1917 when the 2nd Battalion on relief marched out of the line behind their C.O. Lt.-Col. Raikes it consisted of only two officers, the doctor and 73 men—yet it came again.

The Regiment has played a distinguished part in almost all our major campaigns and their record in those extremely difficult peace-keeping operations in which the British Forces have been engaged since the end of the last war has been second to none, particularly in the stinking jungle of Malaya and in the cauldron of Aden.

They were fortunate in another respect: they have a beautiful home. Military barracks are not as a rule noted for their architectural beauty but I will never forget my first visit to their depot at Brecon. I had driven up the valley from Abergavenny and suddenly came on it lying in a most beautiful setting with the Brecon Beacons towering up above. A fitting home, I felt, for those tough little warriors from 'The Valleys' where the hard dangerous life of the miners turns them into some of the best infantry soldiers in the world.

If further proof were needed of the intense Welsh esprit de corps it lies in these pages. After his thirty-seven years service the Regiment has become the author's life and for Jack Adams the writing of this book has obviously been a labour of love. He has succeeded magnificently and I would like to congratulate him on producing a story of which every Welshman should be very very proud.

Preface

'All honour to the Twenty-fourth, of glorious renown. . . .'
(From 'The Noble 24th' by C. C. Anewick; *circa* 1879)

MOST OF THE things that matter in my life have come to me through this Regiment, the 24th, in which it has been my privilege to serve for thirty-seven years. My first acknowledgement, then, must be to the South Wales Borderers (both battalions, but more particularly the 2nd). I am grateful to Lieutenant-General Sir David Peel Yates, K.C.B., C.V.O., D.S.O., O.B.E., the Colonel of the Regiment, for his encouragement, and to Major 'Geo' Egerton, D.L., J.P., the Regimental Secretary, for his phenomenal patience in reading the entire manuscript as well as for the charming manner in which he pointed out my many errors and omissions.

My main reference has been the excellent History by Professor C. T. Atkinson, published by the Cambridge University Press in 1937, but I have consulted many books, some old and now out of print. My thanks go to Lieutenant-Colonel G. A. Brett, D.S.O., O.B.E., M.C., and to Major John Boon (my friend and erstwhile Company Commander) for permission to quote from their books, and to my old comrade and mentor Lieutenant-Colonel Ivor Jarman, M.B.E., for the help and inspiration I received from the Regimental Museum, in the old Barracks at Brecon (which is a veritable panorama of the Regiment's life). Janet Medland, herself the daughter of a serving soldier, typed the manuscript.

My aim has been to produce a readable History: a few
footnotes, no long lists of names or unneccessary dates to
interrupt the free flow of the stirring, sometimes heart-
rending story of the 24th; the reader must judge if I
have succeeded or not. I have only one regret, many
worthwhile tales have been omitted because of lack of space.
The diligent inquirer can, however, fill these gaps by
reading the books referred to in the text; most of them
can be obtained from Regimental Headquarters.

This book is dedicated to all 24th men; past, present and
to come; and to their womenfolk who chose to 'follow the
Drum'.

JACK ADAMS

CHAPTER ONE

1689–1700

'**R**EGIMENTS ARE RAISED in troubled times.' The birth of the 24th Foot was in accordance with this dictum; as indeed was that of most regiments which are now spoken of as 'old'. In the early months of 1689 William and Mary, newly arrived from Holland, reigned uneasily over a Britain still recovering from James II's determined bid to retain the throne of England in the Revolution of 1688.

That revolution led to war with Louis XIV's France (Louis had championed the ill-fated James); and to fight the war it was necessary to provide troops. King William, in the custom of the times, sent off Commissions to the noblemen and landowners who supported his cause. One such Commission went to Sir Edward Dering, 3rd Baronet, of Surrenden, in Kent.

Sir Edward, a rich Member of Parliament, was known locally as the 'Black Devil of Kent', a nickname possibly attributable to his darkly handsome looks. His portrait, credited by some to Peter Lely, hangs in the Officers' Mess of the 1st Battalion of the South Wales Borderers; it shows a hard disdainful mouth and a haughty determined air.

The Commission was acted upon at once. It was dated the 8th of March 1689 and by the 28th of March, the official 'birthday' of the Regiment, the first muster was held. Dering's Regiment, later to be known as the 24th Regiment of Foot (now the South Wales Borderers) became a part of the new Standing Army.

The recruits came mainly from Sir Edward's large

*Sir Edward Dering, Bt.,
first Colonel of the
Regiment, 1689. From a
portrait by Peter Lely.*

estates. His own military experience was limited to the gentlemanly pursuits of a strong supporter of the Crown; he served in the Militia; he was an accomplished swordsman; but he had served in no foreign wars. His brother, Daniel Dering, having commanded a frigate in the Navy, was an experienced campaigner who in 1684 had purchased a Foot Company in Ireland for the reasonable sum of 800 guineas. Sir Edward appointed Daniel to the Lieutenant-Colonelcy of the 24th, knowing that he would bring with him some of the battle-hardened officers who had served with him in the field.

By the 22nd of April the Regiment had moved up to Hoylake in the Wirral peninsula; some nine hundred raw recruits besprinkled with seasoned campaigners who tried to pass on their military skills to the farmhands, labourers and semi-serfs who filled the ranks. In their ill-fitting blue uniforms and their tricorn hats they drilled awkwardly on the stiff clay of the Cheshire fields. They were more intent on avoiding burns from the flaring pans of their antiquated matchlocks than in trying to hit the improvised targets.

The 24th formed part of a miniature army of mixed Horse, Foot and Artillery under the command of General Schomberg, a veteran Huguenot who had been driven into exile from France to the service of William and Mary. He brought with him Dutch and Huguenot contingents who were vastly more experienced than the newly-raised British troops in his small command. Short of money and limited by the lack of efficient equipment and seasoned soldiers he was about to cross to Ireland to subdue the fanatical supporters of James II. The whole country, with the exception of Protestant Ulster, was in rebel hands.

On the 9th of August 1689, the 24th embarked with the rest of the force on the four day voyage to Ireland. They landed on the shores of Belfast Lough and spent an apprehensive first night standing to arms against a Jacobite attack which never came. Schomberg quickly joined up with the smaller force of General Kirke, one of King William's commanders, who had already taken Belfast without a shot being fired.

The combined army moved against the rebel stronghold of Carrickfergus, held by a small but determined garrison. The contingent of artillery accompanying Schomberg's force was manned by inefficient officers; the guns and ammunition were of poor quality; co-operation with the Dutch and Huguenot detachments was almost non-existent. The 24th, whose baptism of fire this was, suffered from the combined carelessness and ignorance. One third of the Regiment were armed only with pikes, they had to carry out their close quarter work against an enemy unharrassed by artillery fire.

It took General Schomberg a week to subdue Carrick-fergus. The dissention between the arrogant but inefficient

British Officers and the campaign-hardened foreign contingents worried him but did not stop his determined drive towards Dublin. He pushed on through Newry towards Dundalk in pursuit of the withdrawing Jacobites. The rebels were committed to a 'scorched earth' policy; they drove the Protestant farmers' cattle and sheep before them, burning the pitiful property of the defenceless peasants with angry impartiality.

But on September 7th, the army ground to a halt at Dundalk, marooned by a shortage of horses and wagons and the dreadful state of the roads; their main supplies were held up at Belfast, three days march behind them. The 24th bivouacked with the others on the peaty bogland. Their winter surtouts, which did duty as greatcoats, lay in store in Belfast; the sentries and picquets endured the chill autumn weather ill-clad while the soft, persistent Irish rain soaked both officers and men indiscriminately.

The foreign contingents, accustomed to foraging for themselves on the European mainland, scoured the desolate countryside for wood and straw, building shacks and shelters against the worsening weather whilst the amateurish British suffered in their damp and leaking tents. This did nothing to heal the breach between the two factions, which was intensified by the high sickness rate afflicting the British. Among the most seriously ill was the Black Devil of Kent. Stricken with a fever which he could not shake off, Sir Edward Dering died on service among the Irish bogs on 17th October, 1689. His brother Daniel, already nominated to succeed to the Colonelcy, was unaware of his death, having gone back to sea in command of a naval vessel.

Schomberg, dismayed by the spreading sickness and unsure of his untrained and untried army, sat tight. He cashiered the Lieutenant-Colonel of Lovelace's Regiment for fomenting bad feeling towards the foreign auxiliaries; he brutally flogged a few deserters 'to encourage the others'; but he refused to break camp even when, emboldened by his inactivity, the rebels came north from Ardee and taunted his troops within range of the British muskets.

The Huguenot general refused to be drawn. He knew that his sick and dispirited soldiers would be outflanked and outmanœuvred, particularly by the Rapparee irregulars who, when they were not looting, formed a valuable guerilla force for the Jacobites. The Rapparees were local Irish Catholics, formed into bands to harass the British, preventing them foraging for much needed fuel. Like Wills-o'-the-wisp, or Viet Cong, they melted away before superior force; but now they were very active. All Schomberg could do was to attempt to alleviate the appalling conditions. He issued coal at the scale of two tons per regiment, trying to eke out the local peat fuel.

Then, in early November, the Jacobites withdrew into winter quarters. General Schomberg thankfully ordered his army to follow suit and the soldiers started their painful march back to Belfast. Over sixteen hundred men had died at Dundalk; eight hundred succumbed on the transports evacuating the sick to England and a further four thousand were to die before the sickness started to subside. At the end of a cruel, dispiriting first year the 24th limped up to Armagh to find quarters against the winter.

Daniel Dering's first action on becoming Colonel of the Regiment was to appoint Samuel Venner as its Lieutenant-Colonel. Venner had transferred from the Dutch service; he was ambitious to improve his position and led the 24th in sorties along the ill-defined border, ranging as far as Omagh, raiding with the British cavalry the enemy's supplies and lines of communication.

In April 1690, when a much needed batch of recruits arrived, they found morale depressingly low. Of some £9,600 owed to the Regiment for pay and equipment only

£4,100 had been paid; food was poor and discipline harsh. The twelve companies of the 24th were widely dispersed between Londonderry, Carlingford and Carrickfergus against quasi-brigands who hid their arms and became sullen peasants as soon as the pressure became too hot to stand (a frustrating position which the Regiment was to encounter centuries later in Palestine and Eritrea, Aden and Malaya).

In June 1691 Daniel Dering died; Venner succeeded him as Colonel of the Regiment, giving the Lieutenant-Colonelcy to Major Alexander Ramsay whose commission in the Regiment dated from March 8, 1689. Shortly after his appointment he led a detachment of the 24th, supported by a body of some 200 cavalry, on a reconnaissance in force towards Sligo. When they reached the outskirts of the town Ramsay found the Ballysclara bridge held by Jacobite partisans under a local leader called Sir Teague O'Regan. Realizing the bridge to be a key position Ramsay attacked and routed the Jacobites, leaving the way clear for Schomberg's following force to converge on Limerick, whose siege was to be the climax of the Irish campaign.

King William had given orders that this last great Jacobite stronghold must be reduced before the autumn rains came. The 24th formed part of the army drawn up on the Clare side of the Shannon, where the Grenadier companies had once more been withdrawn from their regiments to form a separate force to storm the bridge-head into Limerick, which was linked with Connaught by the Thomond bridge.

As the savage assault of the Grenadier companies got under way the rebel defenders broke in disorder. Seeing them stream back towards the bridge leading directly into Limerick the Jacobite officer on duty at the gate panicked. Fearing that the British would force their way into the town on the heels of the fugitives, he raised the drawbridge and left the hapless defenders to be cut down, captured or drowned in the attempt to swim the wide and swollen Shannon. This decisive attack broke the siege. The defenders were granted generous terms, which included a safe passage to France where they were to enrol in the service of Louis XIV. These, the defeated garrison of Limerick, became the forerunners of the famous *émigré* 'Wild Geese', who were to fight for many decades with the French armies. The campaign was over; the 24th left for England, occupying quarters between Bridgewater and Wells in the county of Somerset.

Rumours of a French invasion cut short their stay in the West Country; they moved down to Portsmouth as part of a force of some fourteen battalions, strongly supported by Artillery, under the command of the younger son of the Huguenot General Schomberg who had commanded in Ireland.

After a spate of false alarms they landed at Ostend on the 27th of August 1692; by then the force had grown in size and General Tollemache, 'Talmash' to the troops, led them against Dixmude, which they occupied on the 7th of September. By this time the campaigning season was almost over and they had little hope of taking Dunkirk. A Dutch force took over their garrison from them and they returned to England where they resumed recruiting until quite suddenly, in the spring of 1693, the 24th received orders to exchange its pikes for 'snaphuances' a short firelock designed for shipboard use. All ranks knew that this meant a spell of sea-service; sailors, despite the press-gang, were in short supply and several regiments had been converted into Marines.

For the 24th this sea-change came swiftly, and by May the 23rd they were reported as having 'assumed duties in all respects as seamen', including Naval rationing. The Regiment was split up among several famous ships, including the *Norfolk* and the *Royal William*, forming part of a combined British-Dutch force for the next six months, after which they returned to Portsmouth to spend the winter.

When next they put to sea they resumed their role as infantrymen. A plan was afoot to 'descend upon Brest' and the 24th found itself, shortly after 11 a.m. on the 29th of May 1694, slipping out of harbour in an invasion fleet under the redoubtable Tollemache. The first objective was Camaret Bay and a contemporary account (Green's) gives the sparse orders for the attack. Brigadier Lord Cutts was to lead the way with nine companies of Grenadiers, 'Close behind comes Venner's (the 24th) who will sustain Cutts, then Stuart's who will sustain Venner's, and so every colonel has his regular orders to sustain the other'.

At the landing the French, in some force, held strongly entrenched positions supported by shore batteries. The leading troops were met by an appalling crossfire while the enemy batteries poured in shot at point-blank range; the first wave went down like straw in the wind and the others checked. General 'Talmash' leapt waist-deep into the spray and waded ashore, followed by the bolder members of his staff.

The remainder of the Grenadiers, 'sustained' by the 24th, forced the landing, sheltering with the General and his Staff among the rocks. When he had about 150 men with him, Tollemache rushed the main enemy position, a few yards to his front. The French received them with a terrible, withering fire which killed the officers on either side of Tollemache and decimated the attackers; the General went down with a ball in the thigh and the British were forced to take cover.

Another landing party came up from the flank and with these Tollemache attacked again. Once more he was driven back, this time with even heavier losses. The supporting boats were under heavy fire by now and Tollemache, despite his entreaties, was hustled into one of the Flag-ship's long boats as the French cavalry advanced almost to the water's edge, cutting down all before them.

The attackers withdrew, leaving five hundred, of the six hundred who had landed, dead on the beaches, while a supporting Dutch 30-gun frigate was sunk by the enemy shore batteries. Tollemache died on the way back to Spithead; the ill-timed descent upon Brest had been a total failure.

That winter brought failure also to the aspirations of the Colonel of the 24th. Venner, who had for some time been under suspicion of withholding large sums of money from the Regiment, was at loggerheads with his officers; he was forced to vacate the Colonelcy, and on March the 13th, 1694, at the beginning of the sixth year of the Regiment's life, Louis James Le Vasseur, Marquis de Puisar, became its fourth Colonel.

Le Vasseur was a Huguenot exile who had connections with William's Court. The 24th saw no direct action under him, although they ranged the Mediterranean as Infantry with Admiral Russell, looking for the French. March 1696 saw them billeted around Hereford, Ross and Monmouth, their first contact with the Welsh Border country which they were to know so well in the years to come.

William was feeling the financial pinch of the long war and both sides must have been glad to sign the Peace of Ryswick in September 1697. As the 17th century came to a close the 24th were transferred to the Irish Establishment, narrowly missing disbandment, which was the fate of many of the regiments formed during the previous twenty years.

Reduced in strength, they saw the death of the Marquis de Puisar and for a brief interlude General Seymour became Colonel. Ahead lay the campaigns under Marlborough which were to bring to the 24th the first of its many hard-won Battle Honours.

CHAPTER TWO

1701-1713

UNDER WILLIAM SEYMOUR the 24th saw mainly garrison duty, the strenuous campaigns with John Churchill, 1st Duke of Marlborough were yet to come. In 1701, when the Regiment was in Holland, a number of Officers were sent home to find recruits for two newly raised companies. One of these Officers, a Captain La Coude, encountered in London an Irish soldier of fortune called Peter Drake, who engaged for the 24th after some hard bargaining for a bounty of four guineas, and eightpence a day pay. Unknown to La Coude, Drake had already enlisted in Stuart's Regiment (9th Foot), but hearing that they were to embark for the West Indies (then a fever-ridden 'white man's grave') Drake chose to ship to Holland, to the 24th.

Shortly after joining the Regiment at Gertruydenberg the new recruit got himself wounded in a duel with a fellow Irishman, the Quartermaster of a regiment of Dutch Horse. On rejoining the 24th at Rosendahl Drake had the ill-luck of meeting the very Sergeant of Stuart's who had recruited him for five guineas in London. The Sergeant at once claimed him as a deserter, for which the punishment could be death.

The quick-witted Irishman, having ascertained that the Regiment still wanted him, had the effrontery to plead that he had chosen the 24th because of the better prospect of action in Holland. The Lieutenant-Colonel (Tatton) spoke personally in his favour and Drake was pardoned officially on the understanding that he immediately rejoined the 24th. This he did only to desert a few weeks later after a quarrel with a Sergeant. This time he changed sides, enlisting into the French service. It is interesting to relate that Drake survived Marlborough's campaigns against the French and is on record in 1711 as being once more in a British uniform, serving in Pocock's Scottish regiment alongside the 24th! Unfortunately there is no surviving account of the Regiment's reaction, although Drake probably got the better of the encounter.

On the 12th of February 1702 Marlborough became the Colonel of the 24th. They served under him in the Low Countries during the frustrating period when the great soldier was trying to convince 'obstructive Dutch Deputies, recalcitrant German Princelings and unimaginative colleagues' that the best way of fighting was to engage the enemy head-on. 'Corporal John', as the soldiers called him, commanded the confidence, the affection and the admiration of his troops. One reason for this was the meticulous way in which he attended to detail. Like Montgomery's soldiers in the Eighth Army, Marlborough's men knew that they would want for nothing if their General got his way; and he usually did.

Marlborough's famous march to the Danube, surely one of the most written about expeditions in the course of military history, reflected his genius for administration. The Allied force rendezvoused at Bedburg, not far from Cologne, on May the 7th, 1704, and the next day Corporal John reviewed his army, amongst whom, in the serried ranks of the fourteen British Infantry battalions, stood his own Regiment, the 24th.

It took them some 40 days to complete the 400-mile march, covering 10 to 15 miles a day; the route took them through country varying from monotonous plains to undulating vineyards. At Heidelberg they paused for 4 days before tackling the mountains which divided the Rhine and the Danube. Eventually the leading column snaked down

John Churchill, Duke of Marlborough.

into the Danube valley on the 16th of June 1704 to find Marlborough's allies waiting for him at the Lamm Guesthouse near Giengen, about 15 miles from Ulm. (Incidentally this Inn is still in existence. It was visited by a company of the 1st Battalion South Wales Borderers on the 5th of August 1961, in the course of a march which faithfully followed the footsteps of their Regimental ancestors.)

The expedition had been a complete success. Marlborough's aim was to achieve surprise; the French thought that he might swing right and march through Phillipsburg towards Alsace, and they took no action, giving him time to join forces with his allies, Prince Eugene and the Margrave of Baden. On the 20th of June 1704 the army, fit, well-equipped and eager to fight, were encamped just within sight of the towering Schellenberg.

Marlborough knew that he would have to reduce the

Schellenberg before its already formidable defences were reinforced; this entrenched hill dominated the village of Donauworth with its important bridge. Now the Duke found himself in the rather odd position of sharing command of the Allied Force on alternate days with Prince Louis of Baden. They were men of completely contrasting character; Marlborough, eager for a quick, decisive battle was ever conscious of the value of time; Prince Louis, though a good soldier, was over-methodical and rigid, limited in his ideas and given to the defensive.

The Duke had the command on the 21st of June, and although his army was encamped some 14 miles from the Schellenberg, he decided to act. Before daylight he had his advance guard of thirty squadrons of cavalry and 6,000 picked Infantry (about two companies from each of the forty-five battalions), well on the way. The main body followed two hours later and by 4 p.m. the leading picked detachments of Marlborough's army of some 60,000 men were skirmishing against Marshal d'Arco and his Franco-Bavarian defenders at the foot of the Schellenberg.

Colonel Blood, Marlborough's indefatigable Artillery Commander, had somehow managed to keep his guns up with the leading troops; the preliminary cannonade heralded the start of a struggle as savage and merciless as any seen in the entire campaign. The 24th, two of their companies already committed with the picked detachments, came up with the main body to take part in the counter-attack which finally outflanked the defenders and pushed them off the hill down towards the bridge of boats which spanned the Danube. The Allied Cavalry cut them down as they ran, hastening the panic flight until the bridge collapsed under the weight of the fugitives. Hundreds were drowned, bringing to 9,000 the number of enemy killed or taken prisoner.

The commander of a battalion of French Grenadiers wrote in his memoirs of the British Infantry who 'broke into the charge and rushed at full speed, shouting at the tops of their voices, to throw themselves into our defences. They pressed with the greatest intrepidity up to our parapets. Men were slaying, tearing at the muzzles of guns and at the bayonets which pierced their entrails, crushing under foot their own wounded comrades, and even gouging out their opponents' eyes with their nails'.

The British casualties were heavy. The 24th lost well over half of their men in the picked detachments and had their share of dead in the main assault. The 23rd suffered even more heavily, as did the Guards and the Royal Scots. Marlborough lost no time in crossing the Danube but was too good a soldier to hurl his tired men against the strongly fortified camp at Augsburg, where the enemy had retired to wait for reinforcements from the Rhine.

Impatiently Marlborough awaited the reports of his agents and informers. He was already aware of the importance of the Blenheim position and as soon as he had probed the enemy's strength his army formed up, under cover of the Cavalry, opposite the Franco-Bavarian positions running from Blenheim, on the Danube bank past Oberglau to Lutzingen, where the country was heavily wooded. Marshal Tallard with 20,000 French reinforcements held the right of the enemy line adjoining Blenheim Village while his countryman, Marshal Marsin, with the Elector of Bavaria, held Oberglau and Lutzingen. Facing these last two was Prince Eugene's force; Marlborough, with the rest of the Allied army was drawn up against Tallard, and on Marlborough's left, nearest the Danube, was the Infantry under Major-General Lord Cutts. The 24th, one of five battalions in Rowe's Brigade, were part of the British Infantry force under Cutts when the battle started on the 2nd of August 1704.

Marlborough, to secure his flank, was determined to take Blenheim. Rowe's Brigade, the 24th amongst them, went forward steadily into a hail of enemy fire without discharging a shot. Gaps opened up in the ranks, quickly to be filled by the rear files; as they reached the stockade Rowe plunged his sword into the barricade and only then did they fire their volley. The brigade were vastly outnumbered and the palisades literally swarmed with Frenchmen. The British rushed the enemy defences under murderous fire, Rowe went down and with him many of the leading officers and N.C.O.s. The 24th were pushed back with the rest of the brigade until their right flank was dangerously exposed to the enemy cavalry. They were saved by the Hessians, sent forward at the right time by the watchful Cutts, as the fighting became a confused mêlée of attack and counter-attack.

The British brigades of Ferguson and Hamilton strongly supported Rowe's. The 24th were now involved in a situation which kept them out of Blenheim while hemming the French in. One account (Kane's) depicts the disorder as the twenty-seven French battalions tried to form into battle order inside the congested village, while the British Infantry, now expressly forbidden by Marlborough to press home further attacks, milled around the perimeter warding off bayonet attacks and making minor forays against the French.

With twenty-seven of Tallard's best battalions cooped up inside Blenheim, Marlborough had his way clear. At 4 p.m. he launched his great attack and before long the Allied Cavalry crashed through Tallard's centre, overwhelmed the nine battalions in immediate support and chased his squadrons headlong from the field. Marshal Marsin and the Elector found their flank in danger and hastily tried to evacuate Lutzingen and Oberglau, while Tallard's men in Blenheim village were finally overcome by a British force who broke through into the breach already weakened by the valiant efforts of the 24th and their comrades of Rowe's and Ferguson's.

Marlborough's victory at Blenheim shattered the legend of French invincibility. Casualties were heavy on both sides; Millner wrote that the French sustained a loss of 38,000, three times as many as the Allies. The 24th had some 80 killed, which with their losses at the Schellenberg, accounted for almost a fifth of their strength.

On August the 25th 1704 Marlborough was appointed Colonel of the 1st Foot Guards and Lieutenant-Colonel William Tatton took his place as Colonel of the 24th Foot.

The next two years saw the Regiment marching and counter-marching through the Low Countries. Marlborough, impeded by his reluctant Dutch allies, tried to bring the wily French to battle. It was not until the 12th of May 1706 that Marshal Villeroi, hoping to catch the Duke at a disadvantage, marched to face the British on the marshy ground surrounding the village of Ramillies, in what is now known as Belgium.

The 24th were in Meredith's Brigade, part of a British force of some nineteen battalions and fifteen squadrons of Cavalry. The French defenders of Ramillies were routed after a stubborn resistance which turned into a headlong retreat ending in heavy losses for Villeroi. British casualties were light and the 24th marched on with their allies to take part in the siege of Ostend. The reduction of the city proved easier than was expected and Marlborough was able to secure shorter lines of communication to his English base.

The following year was a disappointing one for the Allies. Bad weather and reverses in Spain and Southern Germany kept Marlborough short of much-needed reinforcements and deprived him of the numerical superiority which could have forced the French to battle. In consequence it was not until June the 30th 1708 that the 24th again took part in a major action.

This was at Oudenarde, on the River Scheldt, where

their brigade was commanded by Gilbert Primrose, who had recently succeeded Tatton as Colonel of the Regiment. Marlborough was still smarting from the losses of Bruges and Ghent; he was anxious to confront the French and spurred his troops to such efforts that one British Officer, writing of the approach to the battle, said that 'the soldiers had not seen bed for five days or eaten a hot meal for seven'. The French attacked first and desperate close-quarter fighting developed, the enemy being beaten back from breastwork to breastwork until, in the failing light, Marlborough's Cavalry, under the Dutch General Auver-querque, turned the French flank.

The British Infantry, two brigades strong, supported by the Cavalry under Prince Eugene, exploited this success until the hard-pressed French broke in disorder. 'Had we two hours more daylight,' Marlborough wrote afterwards, 'they would have been entirely destroyed.' But his ambitious plans to march straight into France were frustrated by his Dutch allies and the Duke reconciled himself to besieging Lille, then the chief bulwark of French Flanders. Five British battalions were engaged in the siege, including the 24th, who lost 69 killed and 208 wounded before the city fell on the 4th of October, 1708.

The 24th had their fill of sieges, large and small, during the remaining years of their service in the Netherlands. The long winter of 1708 was exceptionally hard and rigorous. The Allies and the French quarrelled and bickered over the Treaty made at Ryswick and the terms of settlement. The French General Villars, although boastful and truculent, had restored the discipline and the spirit of King Louis' army, assembling a force of some 80,000 in a determined effort to hold Marlborough before the strong and skilfully planned defences in front of Malplaquet.

The battle opened at 7 a.m. on the 31st of August 1709. The 24th came under the command of Lord Orkney, facing a French force inferior in number but protected by formidable entrenchments. The battle lasted until the 11th of September when the Allies gained an indisputable victory. No clear casualty list of the Regiment is available for this battle although the Allied losses were some 20,000, almost twice that of the French.

Marlborough now wanted to capture Douai, one of the last really important fortresses in the barrier between France and the Netherlands. Douai was extremely strongly defended, part of the land around it was flooded, and canals and rivers made it difficult to approach. The two months' long siege took a heavy toll of the 24th and the other seven British battalions, and when the Governor of Douai 'beat for a parley' on the 14th of June 1710 the Regiment had lost 36 killed and 157 wounded.

The 24th stayed on with Marlborough until Queen Anne, turning against the Whigs and the war, brought his campaigning to an end. The Regiment had gained great renown, although it was not until 1882 that the battle honours Blenheim, Ramillies, Oudenarde and Malplaquet were emblazoned on its Colours. Before the Spanish Succession the British Army had no very special place among European armies, but during William III's reign and on into Queen Anne's, Marlborough had succeeded in establishing the great traditions which the 24th were to assist in enhancing in the decades to come.

The Regiment left the Netherlands on June the 24th 1713, taking with them to their new station in Ireland the knowledge that in their first really serious experience of Continental warfare they had emerged with enduring fame.

CHAPTER THREE

1714-1742

THERE ARE PERIODS in the history of the 24th when the mists of Ireland obscure the written record; when out of the 'Celtic Twilight' there emerges tradition unsupported by hard fact. For instance, were the 24th ever in Scotland during the rising of 1715?

Tradition says that they were. But there is no record of the Regiment arriving in North Britain, or of its continuing presence there. Part of the obscurity can be put down to the destruction of the Irish Records in the Rebellion of 1916; this lack of documentary support irked C. T. Atkinson, the Regiment's main Historian, who suggests that the 24th might have been wrongly deprived of the Hanoverian 'White Horse' badge, which was given as a distinction to those regiments who helped to suppress 'the Fifteen'.

But we can be certain that for some twenty-five years from 1713, apart from two short spells in England, the Regiment served on the Irish Establishment. These decades under the first two Georges must have been desperately dull after the glorious Continental campaigns of Marlborough's wars. True, there were barracks for the soldiers (whereas there were none in England), but the harsh, severe discipline; the low pay; the crime, drunkenness and brutality attracted recruits of low character and poor physique. Desertion was rife. The Colonels of Regiments, the nominal Commanding Officers, were usually Generals who as often as not were away on military expeditions or even engaged in some post to augment their regimental pay. The actual command was delegated to the Lieutenant-Colonel.

There was no military Commander-in-Chief; the direction of the Army down to the most petty details of minor administration was in the hands of a civilian, the Secretary of War. Yet, despite this, most regiments preserved a degree of efficiency and steadiness in war which moved continental observers to astonished admiration.

Colonel Gilbert Primrose died in 1717. He was succeeded as Colonel by Thomas Howard, who came from Wade's (the 33rd, later Duke of Wellington's) and who stayed with the 24th for twenty years, bequeathing them the nickname of 'Howard's Greens', the grass-green facings being still worn on the red mess jackets of the officers.

In 1719 the Vigo Expedition must have come as a welcome break from the monotony of Irish garrison life, and this time the 24th were to fight on the side of the French against the Spanish. The Regiment sailed as part of a force of 9,000 under the command of Lord Cobham against the strongly held port of Corunna, on the coast of Spain. The fleet changed course after learning that Corunna was well prepared and alert, and on the evening of the 29th of September Cobham landed his grenadier companies on the coast near Vigo to secure a practically unopposed beachhead.

The main force disembarked the next day with the object of destroying the vast amount of war material known to be stored at Vigo. As the British reached the outskirts of the town the Spaniards spiked their guns and retired into the fortified citadel, offering stiff resistance which forced Cobham to bring up mortar and siege guns. By the 10th of October the garrison had capitulated.

Although rumours reaching Madrid had magnified the small British force into a massed invasion army, Cobham realized that his troops stood no chance against the strongly held ports of Corunna or Ferrol. He hastily embarked the most serviceable enemy guns and as much ammunition as he could safely carry, putting the vast stores at Vigo and Ponte Vedra to the torch. On the 26th October Cobham sailed for home after inflicting, at the price of less than 300 British casualties (including 'those that fell by the Vine') a blow to Spanish morale and prestige out of all proportion to the cost.

For the 24th it was back to Ireland, where they remained, except for short sojourns in England around 1727 and 1734, until the spring of 1740. In 1737 the long tenure of Thomas Howard came to an end. Major-General The Right Hon. Thomas Wentworth succeeded him; and under Wentworth, at San Juan de Cartagena, some of the saddest pages in the Regiment's long history were written.

Once more the Spaniards were to be the main enemy. The Anglo-Spanish War, sometimes called 'the war of Jenkins' Ear', had flared up because of the grant to England of trading rights with what is now known as the West Indies. Relations were already strained on account of our occupation of Gibraltar and Minorca; at the end of 1739 the two countries were openly at war.

A strange situation existed. England hesitated to attack Spain because of her massive army, whilst Spain could not invade England in the face of our large navy. But in the West Indies Spain was vulnerable. A force was assembled in the Isle of Wight under the command of Lord Cathcart, who had chosen General Wentworth, the Colonel of the 24th as his second-in-command; the destination was Cartagena.

It was late October 1741 before the large fleet of transports got under way. On embarkation the 24th had a negligible sick list but by the time the scattered ships had reached the island of Dominica only 418 out of 1,000 men were still effective.

Many of the force had died from their long incarceration in the small, overcrowded vessels; scurvy was rife, food had almost gone and water was dangerously low. Among the dead was Lord Cathcart, who succumbed to 'a bloody flux' after a fortnight's illness. This was a sore blow to the British because Wentworth, though an able, even willing, subordinate, had neither the calibre nor the will to successfully seize the responsibility so unexpectedly thrust upon him. The fleet reassembled and pushed on to Jamaica, where they arrived on January the 7th 1741 to find the fire-eating Admiral Vernon itching to get at the Spaniards. Vernon had recruited four battalions of Americans (presumably from the North American colonies) but had forgotten to provide for rations or supplies for them, thus putting the 24th and their comrades in arms on even shorter 'commons'.

Then, to complicate matters, news arrived that war with France was imminent. There was a French squadron at San Domingo; Vernon realized that he would have to move fast if he was to avoid the risk of being descended upon by the French force whilst attacking the Spaniards. Fortunately for him, the French (perhaps thinking that the British fleet was directed against them) sailed for the open Atlantic before the Admiral's ships reached San Domingo.

As he sailed up the Caribbean Sea Vernon briefed General Wentworth on the difficulties of the approaches to Cartagena. Situated in semi-tropical latitudes on the north coast of South America (in what is now called Colombia), the town was of great importance to the Spanish. The Captain-General of the Indies lived there and it was their main administrative centre.

Its completely land-locked harbour was surrounded by shoal water; there was one entrance at Boca Chica ('Little Mouth') eight miles from the town. Guarding the northern approaches to the 'Little Mouth' were three forts; Fort San Luis, sometimes known as 'Boca Chica Castle', mounting 80 guns; Fort San Felipe and Fort San Jago.

Admiral Vernon put his plan into action. On March the 9th, whilst other ships made a feint against the town, his men-of-war bombarded Forts San Felipe and Jago. Within two hours the guns had been silenced; the detached grenadier companies under Major Hamon of the 24th made an assault landing and gained a foothold near some thick woods about a mile from the first objective, Fort San Luis. Admiral Vernon wanted an immediate attack, Wentworth was more cautious: 'Mr. Vernon,' he said, 'is altogether unacquainted with the land service, he looks to the end without the means.'

It is possible that the careful, methodical Wentworth made his first error at that time. The humid, fever-ridden climate; the thick tropical vegetation; all pointed to the urgency for speed, many of the soldiers were already ill and hundreds were to die of sickness before the campaign ended. The soldiers waited for two days in the burning sun, tentless and ill equipped. Then, with hastily landed guns and supplies, they advanced under cover to within half a mile of Fort San Luis to find that the ground to their front had been cleared of vegetation to give the fort a good field of fire.

Artillery was manhandled forward and Wentworth opened up on the fort, supported from the sea by a bombardment from five men-of-war. A breach was made by the land batteries and, in the evening, the grenadier companies formed up for the assault. As they waited on the start line the British batteries poured a charge of round shot into the opening followed up by a devastating volley of grape shot 'which obliged the enemy's sentinels to retire'.

As the grenadiers rushed through the smoke into the small breach they failed to see the white flag go up, nor did they understand the significance of the sudden drum-roll of the 'chamade' which the Spaniards were beating as a signal for a parley. When the grenadiers showed no sign of checking their headlong attack the enemy, thinking that no quarter would be given, beat a panic retreat which spread to the neighbouring Spanish batteries.

The British swarmed unopposed into Fort San Luis and from there went on to cut the boom defences guarding the harbour. The rest of the forts around Boca Chica were subdued and the way into the harbour was clear. The first objective had been overcome at a cost of less than 150 casualities, but this was outweighed by 250 deaths from disease and an ever-growing list of more than 600 sick. Among the battle casualties was Lieutenant-Colonel Sandford of the 24th; Major Hamon, who had commanded the grenadier companies in the first assault, was promoted in his place.

As soon as Vernon had manœuvred his fleet into the harbour the two forts defending the inner anchorage were attacked. The Spaniards evacuated them before the assault went in and as soon as the entrance was cleared bomb-ships were taken into the inner harbour ready for the attack on Cartagena. Wentworth proceeded to tackle this in three stages. First, to land at La Quinta, about three miles east of the town; then to subdue Fort San Lazare, which stood on a 'pimple' 70 feet above the plain within gunshot of Cartagena; lastly, the assault on the town itself.

Worried by his enormous losses through sickness, Wentworth asked Admiral Vernon for reinforcements from the Infantry retained on board the naval ships in lieu of marines; even the Americans eventually landed, making the force at La Quinta up to some 5,000 men. On April the 5th the first contingent moved against Fort Lazare. Spearheaded by grenadiers it consisted of the 15th, 36th, 24th, 34th and Marines, in that order, moving along a track which ran through wooded country for about a mile to a high feature called Madre di Popa, and it was here that the first serious resistance was encountered. The advance guard commander soon overcame it and pressed on to within half a mile of San Lazare before orders from the over-cautious Wentworth recalled him to La Quinta, where the force remained, despite Vernon's protests while guns, stores, and more Americans were disembarked. The Admiral, worried about the approaching rainy season, finally stung Wentworth into action by offering to storm Fort San Lazare with his own sailors.

The plan was to assault simultaneously from both north and south. A backing labour force of a thousand Americans were to follow up with scaling ladders, woolpacks for filling up ditches, and reserves of ammunition, whilst Wolfe's Marines, 450 strong, were held as a reserve to support either assault party. At 2 a.m. on the 9th of April, the grenadier companies approached the Southern side, led by Colonel Wynyard of the 4th Marines. The 24th and the 15th, who had been reinforced from Bland's and Cavendish's, moved quietly to the Northern base of the 'pimple'. Unfortunately, the officer who had reconnoitred Wynyard's route failed to turn up, the grenadiers lost direction and found themselves clawing their way up a steep slope on their hands and knees. Coming to the top, blown and exhausted, they were mown down by a close-quarter blast from the enemy, who were less than 30 yards away.

The 24th, on the northern side, found themselves enmeshed in a maze of defences, where the early daylight exposed them to small-arms fire from the town of Cartagena. Grant gallantly led them up into the perimeter defences, forcing a way into the fort, continually calling for facines and ladders from the support party. There was no reply, the Americans had bolted. Untrained, officered by men described as 'a composition of all the banditti these colonies afford', the support party threw down their loads and disappeared into the dawn.

For some reason the marines in reserve were not

brought up. Ammunition quickly ran out; enemy troops appeared from the town, forming up for a counter attack on the fort; many of the officers had fallen, there was nothing for it but to withdraw to La Quinta. That night 40 officers and 600 men had fallen, of these 131 came from the 24th. The dejected and dispirited troops, with no hospital accommodation and few medical stores, were in danger of being wiped out by sickness. Wentworth, all confidence gone, abandoned the enterprise and sailed for Jamaica on the 26th of April, 1741.

For the next year the British force remained in the West Indies, making an ineffectual attempt to capture Cuba, followed by a descent upon Panama which was defeated by the gathering rains. In October 1742 the ill-fated campaign ended. In terms of lives it had cost the 24th a dozen officers and some 800 men; the gallant attempt on San Lazare had proved only that 'a bloody war or a sickly season' favoured promotion for those who survived.

CHAPTER FOUR

1743-1763

THE 24TH HAD been on duty in England for three years when, in 1745, the Jacobite rising in support of Bonnie Prince Charlie took the country by surprise. They remained in England, mainly in the West Country, until rumours of a French invasion moved them east to Newbury and Reading.

Thomas Wentworth, who had been campaigning in the Netherlands, was succeeded as Colonel of the Regiment in June 1745 by Daniel Houghton, the first Colonel to be denied the honour of putting his crest upon the Colours. For in September 1743 a Royal warrant had set the number of colours to be carried by each regiment at two; one to bear the 'Great Union' of the crosses of St. George and St. Andrew and the other to be of the colour of the facings (in the case of the 24th, green) with the Union in the top corner nearest the pike. This was more to identify the Regiment with the monarch, although it was still 'owned' by the Colonel.

On March the 29th 1746, the 24th were ordered to Scotland. Arriving after the battle of Culloden they spent a short time in helping to subdue the last lingering resistance of the rebellion, then together with most of the other regiments, they began the arduous task of building the military roads which were to open up the Highlands to pacification. During this time Houghton died and was succeeded as Colonel by William Kerr, Earl of Ancram.

The Regiment moved back to England in September 1749, where three years later another change of Colonels

*Lt.-Gen. the Honourable
Edward Cornwallis,
1713–1776, by Sir Joshua
Reynolds.*

occurred. Ancram went back to his old regiment (the 11th Dragoons) and the Hon. Edward Cornwallis came in from the 40th Foot to find that regulations now required the Regiment's title to be written as 'The 24th (Cornwallis's) Regiment of Foot', a further weakening of the Colonel's proprietary power which eventually led to the use of numbers only as a reference.

Over the past years relations with France had deteriorated. Gradually, as war had flared with the Spanish over trade with the New World, so war with France became imminent because of the British colonists' commercial ambitions in the French territories in North America. In June 1755 Admiral Boscawen attempted to board French military transports in the Atlantic, and war became inevitable.

The 24th were then in Minorca. Since June 1752 they had helped to garrison this tactically valuable island, with its splendid harbour, in company with three other battalions. The local inhabitants were hostile and obstructive;

as a result fresh meat and fish to supplement the ration
was hard to come by but, by and large, life was pleasant
enough.

The main defences were centred around Port Mahon
and it was here, at Fort St. Philip, that the Regiment were
soon to see action. Because of invasion scares in England
Minorca had been neglected by the powers that be; in
consequence, when the Duc de Richelieu arrived with
15,000 French troops off the western end of the island on
April the 17th, 1756, there was little the few defenders
could do to stop him landing.

A private of the
Grenadier company, 1751.

The Lieutenant-Governor of the island was Blakeney, a veteran of 82 who had served under King William. He proceeded to plan the defences with resolution and skill, pulling the 24th and most of the garrison back into the strongly defended Fort St. Philip where a system of underground galleries cut into the rock formed the basement of a formidable fortification system. Four bastions gave all round fire, supported by an outer ring of redoubts and 'lunettes' (crescent-shaped defences), which ran up to the end of the rocky promontory on which St. Philip stood. On the left, as one looked out to sea, ran the deep finger of an inlet called St. Stephen's Cove, on the far side of which was a strongly built outpost, called Marlborough Redoubt, covering the entrance.

Blakeney's covering screen withdrew into Fort St. Philip as soon as it was certain that the French were marching on Mahon. Using what may now seem odd protocol the defenders sent out the Drum-Major of the 24th 'in military form, to demand the reason of the French King's troops landing in a hostile manner in His Majesty's island of Minorca' (for there had been no formal declaration of war). The Drum-Major came back to tell them that Richelieu had stated that England could not seize French ships at sea with impunity. Then, it is recorded, 'further compliments were exchanged' including a present of fruit from the French, acknowledged by Blakeney with a gift of six bottles of British beer. With these unusual formalities out of the way the serious business soon began.

The French started to erect siege batteries in the suburbs adjoining the landward side of St. Philip. This action brought heavy fire from the nearest redoubt, Queen's, and the enemy pulled back among the sheltering buildings of the suburbs. On May the 8th the French got two batteries going; following up that evening with an attack on the Marlborough Redoubt by 500 men under the command of Prince Louis of Würtemberg. The tiny garrison (50 men of the 24th), beat off the attack, causing the Prince and his men to 'retire with some loss and great precipitation'.

The defenders used the tunnels and redoubts to great advantage, causing the French to expend a lot of ammunition to little effect. On May the 19th Blakeney's spirits were raised by the sighting of a British fleet rounding the south-east end of the island in the morning light. Hopes were dashed when the wind freshened and the fleet sailed on without a boat being lowered or a message passed. It later transpired that the fleet commander, the controversial Admiral Byng, after an inconclusive encounter with French men-of-war, had decided against landing reinforcements at Minorca. For this he was subsequently courtmartialled and shot (the French, perhaps with some truth, held that the execution was carried out 'to encourage the others').

This let-down for the defenders was followed by a month of constant and heavy battering, continuing on the 27th of June with a bombardment which opened up the way for the final assault. Morale had been shaken by the gradual whittling away of the defences, first the Anstruther battery fell, and then Kane's Redoubt which covered the West Bastion of the fort nearest the suburbs from which the main attack came. The wine ration was halved; then, cruel blow, the aquadente (brandy) 'was entirely taken away'. The Queen's Redoubt, next to Kane's, was overwhelmed despite the valiant efforts of the King's Own. This did the French no good, however, because as soon as the enemy were well into Queen's the defenders exploded a series of mines which blew up three full companies of grenadiers.

Across St. Stephen's Cove a captain and 50 men of the 24th were assailed on all sides by the enemy du Roi and Bretagne regiments, some 700 strong, who withdrew with heavy losses after their leader, the Comte de Lannion, was wounded. But already that day the defenders had lost enough men to endanger the outposts. The French had got into the subterranean passages; the hope of relief was remote, to continue the struggle would have meant slaughter for the 'four brave battalions'. Blakeney decided to capitulate.

He reckoned without the ordinary soldiers, who determined to fight on, had to be restrained by their officers with threats and menaces when the 'parley' was beaten on the drums. The Duc de Richelieu was impressed. His terms, giving due respect to the 24th and their compatriots, included: 'the full honours of war, to march out with firelocks on their shoulders, drums beating, colours flying, twenty cartridges for each man'. Not only did he arrange for them to embark at once for Gibraltar on French transports, he also released all prisoners and made it plain that they were free to serve anywhere without having to be exchanged. The Duc's handsome gesture might have been prompted by foresight, for Admiral Hawke, having defeated the covering French fleet, met the returning garrison ten days out of Mahon. Richelieu by then was safely in Toulon.

No excuse need be made for the unsuccessful defence of Minorca. The small garrison had inflicted heavy losses on a force three or four times stronger than their own. Upholding the finest traditions of the British Army they had fought on until, against their own wishes but at the dictates of reason, the old but gallant Blakeney rightly yielded to overwhelming force.

In November 1756 the Regiment reached Portsmouth from Gibraltar to receive a tumultuous welcome, richly deserved.

That same year, while the 24th was still at Gibraltar, orders had been given for fifteen regiments each to form a second battalion. The quarrel between France and Britain had widened into an imperial struggle between the

Prussian King, Frederick the Great, and Maria Teresa of Austria, strongly supported by Louis XV of France. Hanover, part of George II's British dominions, was directly threatened, and the scene was set for the Seven Years War.

The 24th was one of the fifteen regiments selected for expansion; its 2nd Battalion was recruited mainly from the area of Lincolnshire, moving into Leicestershire to join the 1st Battalion which had arrived there in May 1757. The 1st Battalion had recently been inspected at Derby by its old Colonel, the Earl of Ancram, who had been succeeded by Cornwallis in 1752. It is worth examining some of the interesting facts that Atkinson culled from the report.

There were 620 men on parade; 37 sick, 43 recruiting, 39 on leave, amounting to all but 41 of the full establishment. All were English excepting 12 Scots, 22 Irish and 3 foreigners (in those days Welshmen were counted as English). They were a pretty formidable lot; 29 were over 6 feet tall, 96 over 5 feet 10 inches and only 6 below 5 feet 6 inches. Seven were over fifty years old, 113 over forty, 391 over thirty and only 2 under twenty. Nearly 400 of them could claim ten years service and upwards, 26 had more than twenty years. Only 90 were recent enlistments.

There is no such report on the 2nd Battalion; it was to stay part of the 24th Foot for a brief two years before becoming a regiment in its own right (the 69th now, with the 41st, the Welch Regiment).

Meanwhile the British Government, under Pitt, decided to mount a series of expeditions against French coastal concentrations, hoping to destroy war material and to keep employed enemy troops which might otherwise be used against Hanover or the British North American Colonists. (Pitt did not favour direct British participation in Continental wars.) Rochefort, St. Malo, Cherbourg and St. Cast were attacked without any great success. The 24th must have been glad to return to the Isle of Wight after weeks of tossing on the choppy seas of the Channel and the Bay of Biscay in small, smelly troop transports.

Pitt was then forced to change his policy. Frederick the Great's crushing defeat by the Austrians at Kunersdorf in the late summer of 1759 resulted in heavy pressure on the British Government to augment its troops in Germany. Amongst the six battalions sent was the 24th, made up to a strength of 1,034 all ranks; this brought the force in Westphalia up to over 22,000 men. At the end of May 1760 the Regiment joined the British contingent of Ferdinand of Brunswick's army of Hessians, Hanoverians and Brunswickers.

Two months later, under command of Ferdinand's nephew, they saw their first action against the French at Corbach. The Hanoverians were outnumbered; a major disaster seemed imminent, but the steady, firm discipline of the 24th and the 33rd under General Howard and the 50th and 51st under General Griffin enabled the Prince to extricate his shaken force in the nick of time. 'They showed the greatest eagerness to engage,' wrote the famous Marquis of Granby, 'and in the retreat the greatest firmness and discipline.' They stood under the severe cannonade as if made of stone; the French Cavalry made no impression upon them.

These sterling qualities stood them in good stead in the victories of Warberg, Clostercamp and Vellinghausen. The British contingent formed the backbone of Ferdinand's Allied Forces during the three years of that hard campaign. When the Peace of Paris was signed in 1763, Hanover was out of peril. But another far-reaching result was the withdrawal of French troops from Canada, allowing the control of the whole of North America to pass to Britain.

CHAPTER FIVE

1764–1802

THE REGIMENT GARRISONED Gibraltar for the next few years, then moved once more to Ireland. Again the 'Irish mist' supervenes; records are difficult to trace, the Army List and other sources give only details of changes amongst the officers. One major change was that of the Colonel of the Regiment. In January 1776 after holding the post for twenty-four years Cornwallis died, to be replaced by William Taylor who had been the Lieutenant-Colonel of the 9th (Royal Norfolk).

A few years earlier, as the result of the successful skirmishing and outpost work of the light troops during the Westphalian campaign, a 'Light Company' had been brought into being. Like the grenadier company it consisted of active and intelligent men specially trained for the job. It took the left of the line (the grenadiers held the right) and it had two Lieutenants but no Ensign. When the 24th were drafted to Canada in April 1776 these skirmishers proved invaluable in the semi-guerilla warare which followed.

The 'Boston Tea Party' had been over for some three years when the Regiment arrived at Quebec in June 1776. The American rebels who invaded Canada under Benedict Arnold had been pushed south from Quebec; Sir Guy Carleton, Governor of Canada, and Commander-in-Chief, now had great plans for the newly arrived force. Simon Fraser, the Lieutenant-Colonel of the 24th, was promoted and given a special 'Advance' Brigade consisting of his own battalion, commanded by the senior Major, Grant, and two picked detachments from the grenadiers and the light companies.

After some preliminary skirmishing along the St. Lawrence River (where the 24th succeeded in driving some 300 Americans into swampland, where they surrendered) the main force reached Sorel, already evacuated by the enemy, and turned south along the line of the River Richelieu towards Lake Champlain. It was early October before sufficient locally constructed gun-boats were available, but Benedict Arnold's flotilla was soon defeated and Fraser pushed on to Crown Point, a bare 12 miles from Ticonderoga.

Governor Carleton now decided that enough had been done for the season. It was well into October; a Canadian winter had to be faced, lines of communication were stretched and inadequately secured. The entire force withdrew to the Northern end of Lake Champlain to winter quarters, the 24th occupying a pleasant village called Verchere, near Montreal, overlooking the St. Lawrence. The soldiers were issued with 'blanket coats and leggins as well as fur caps and mittins', which seems to have kept the sick rate down. Very few died that winter, but among those that did was Lieutenant Pennington of the 24th, whose place as Adjutant was taken by one Sergeant Calladine.

While the Regiment was resting the Governor was being subjected to a barrage of criticism over his failure to push on to Ticonderoga. They charged Carleton with building useless fortifications; with being tardy over his boat building (because almost all movement was by water) and most bitterly with giving the Americans time to recruit backwoodsmen and sharpshooters to swell the rebel ranks. But he was a good administrator as well as an above average soldier; he must have had good reasons for his decisions. His force was new to the country, the expected 'native' contingent of Canadians, forecasted to build up to substantial numbers, was never more than a handful; while the few Indians recruited were unreliable and of poor quality. The country was rugged and thickly wooded, with few tracks. Lines of advance were along rivers and lakes; ideal country for the guerilla tactics at which the enemy were expert.

As the new campaigning season approached, Carleton and his commanders studied the British plan of action, centred on the army of Sir William Howe, whose base was at New York. Essentially it followed a line running north along the course of the Hudson river to Albany, to which Howe would advance with an offensive force of some 10,000 men; leaving 5,000 to hold New York and a further 8,000 to threaten Philadelphia, thus occupying the main American army. The Canadian contingent, under General Burgoyne, would move south towards Albany, where both forces would eventually link. Burgoyne had 5,000 British, 3,500 Germans and the 'handful' of Canadians and Indians already mentioned.

But the plan was modified by Howe, who switched his main force against Philadelphia. When, months later, detailed orders arrived in Canada via Whitehall they stated, surprisingly, that Sir William Howe would put himself under command of General Burgoyne when their respective forces met at Albany. Nothing was said about the switch to Philadelphia. This change of plan had a significant effect on the later events at Saratoga and the battle for Bemis Heights.

By June the 11th 1777 Burgoyne's force had concentrated on the Western shore of Lake Champlain about 20 miles from Ticonderoga. Fraser with his advanced Brigade pushed on towards this strongly fortified settlement and secured the high ground of Mount Hope, a mile or so from it. On the 4th of July he had taken the Saw Mills South of Ticonderoga, going on to seize Sugar Loaf Hill, which overlooked both the settlement and the high ground near it, which was regarded as the key of the defences. Then, to the consternation of the enemy, the British hauled some guns to the top of the Sugar Loaf, a feat which the Americans had regarded as impossible and which now put them at Burgoyne's mercy. On the night of the 5/6th July they cut their losses and evacuated Ticonderoga in haste, leaving some 80 guns and a mass of stores.

Fraser followed them east towards Skenesborough, hurriedly collecting the 24th and the rest of his Brigade as he advanced. At 3 a.m. on the 7th of July, the enemy were caught and attacked at their breakfasts by two companies of the 24th under Major Grant. In the mêlée Grant was shot by a sniper, and the 24th, vastly outnumbered, were fighting back to back until the arrival of the Light Infantry. Fraser put in a grenadier battalion to prevent the Americans retreating, but the rebels came at them with 'clubbed arms' as if to surrender. As soon as the grenadiers came into the open the Americans opened fire, but before they could consolidate their ill-gotten gains General Reidesel's Germans arrived and turned the enemy defence into a route, leaving 200 killed, 600 wounded and 230 prisoners.

At Skenesborough Fraser halted with Burgoyne's main force while ammunition and supplies came up. This un-avoidable pause gave the Americans time to recover from the shock caused by the loss of Ticonderoga. Rumours that General Burgoyne was going to flood the countryside with 'rogue' Indians helped to bring hundreds of formid-able, forest-trained fighting men to the enemy cause. By the time the British had pushed down the Hudson to Saratoga the enemy had mustered a force of 10,000 men on the strongly fortified Bemis Heights, some 200 feet above the river. On September the 17th Burgoyne estab-lished a camp on the river about 4 miles from the Heights; the country between was broken and thickly wooded, leading to a deep ravine which protected the American position.

Artillery was obviously going to be a vital factor in the reduction of this fortress. Burgoyne planned to move his guns (protected by Reidesel's Germans), along the left flank, following the line of the river. The centre column of the force consisted of four British battalions, while Fraser, with one company of the 24th acting as advance guard, took his force well out to the right flank, hoping to come out at the head of the Mill Creek ravine. He would then join with the centre covering the passage of the ravine by the all-important guns, and the Germans.

General Gates, the American Commander, did not wait for the threat to develop, he attacked the centre column in force. Fraser detached the Light Infantry and two companies of the 24th, who attacked the enemy flank so savagely that the Americans broke off and the centre was slowly able to move forward.

Gates then attacked Fraser's column, checking the fierce counter-attack of five companies of the 24th and forcing them to bring up two extra companies before they could rally enough strength to push the enemy back, leaving fifty of their own (24th) men dead upon the ground. The Americans, probing for a weak spot, then swung against the centre, but Burgoyne was able to bring his guns and the Germans up on the left and drive them back.

Dusk had fallen, casualties had been heavy; one regiment, the 62nd, had lost half its effectives; with the darkness came a lull in the fighting. That night (the 19th of September) Burgoyne praised the exhausted troops for their stubborn fighting, Fraser's force coming in for special mention. But, as Atkinson points out, it was a Pyrrhic conquest, a stop-gap victory to be paid for dearly in the coming days.

The British force consolidated its ground around Freeman's Farm overlooking the ravine, a cannon's shot from the enemy. There they stayed for the next fortnight trying to improve their position, whilst rebel recruits flocked to

Gate's colours. Had Burgoyne known the true state of the British strategy it is possible that he may have made good his retreat, for at this stage the enemy were in no condition to press him. But he was convinced that his duty was to prevent Gates joining up with the main American forces further south. He later wrote that he saw the role of his army as 'to be hazarded and devoted' to the prevention of Gates joining Washington, even to the loss of his own retreat to Canada; and this was soon to happen.

The American right flank was now practically unassailable, their augmented strength enabling them to build up strong outposts in a short space of time. The British position was deteriorating daily; the constant fire, day and night, caused many of the Canadians and the Indians to desert. Ammunition and rations were short, the men were packed so closely that sleep was difficult to come by.

On October the 7th Burgoyne made a desperate move around the enemy's left flank, hoping to dislodge the Americans and pave the way for an unmolested retreat. This force had 1,500 men, including the 24th, with 10 guns; but despite the wooded country they were soon detected and attacked frontally by the rebels. At the same time another American, General Morgan, stormed the British right, and Burgoyne now realized that he must fall back. The 24th and the Light Infantry took post to cover the retirement, but the Germans in the centre began to waver causing Fraser to rush the 24th to that sector with the Light Infantry to restore the balance. As he did so he was hit by a sniper and with his death the Regiment lost one of its finest officers.

His last action enabled the British to retire in some semblance of order to their defence lines, but not without the sacrifice of six guns and many men. In the face of repeated fierce attacks by the enemy the position became quite untenable. Burgoyne realized that he must now re-

The burial of Brigadier-Gen. Simon Fraser, mortally wounded at Stillwater near Saratoga on October 7th, 1777, when in command of the 'Advance Corps' of General Burgoyne's Army.

treat before the Americans got between him and Fort Edward. This was twenty miles away; to attain mobility it would be necessary to jettison the guns and leave the wounded behind. The 24th, with the rest of poor Fraser's Brigade, were detailed as rearguard, and on the night of the 8th of October the half-starved, weary and bedraggled soldiers moved off into the rain-soaked dusk.

Harassed by snipers, the force was overtaken by the fast-moving Americans, who succeeded in occupying the ground between them and Fort Edward in such numbers that surrender became inevitable. General Gates consented to change his demand for 'unconditional surrender' when he found that Burgoyne would rather attempt to fight on than accept ignominious terms. The troops were allowed to travel to Boston to embark for England on the condition that they would not again serve in America during the war.

The hard campaign had ended in disaster, though it was three years before the American War of Independence finally ended with the defeat of the British General Cornwallis at Yorktown in 1781. The 24th had lived up to the example of their ancestors of Marlborough's days; hard-fighting and hard-marching, bearing the brunt in attack and retreat; no blame for the disaster could be attached to them. The Regiment was dispersed but not defeated; they would rise again.

In England the recruiting company which had remained behind was tramping the country. Captain Pilmor, who was in command, had been at Saratoga and so had Captains Verchild and Jones. An Inspection Return of July 1784 shows the Regiment as being 260 strong, more than half of them recruits. The Lieutenant-Colonel was named England, a huge man of whom the Duke of York is said to have exclaimed: 'England! England! Great Britain, by God!' Among the other officers was the same Calladine who had become Adjutant from the rank of Sergeant in Canada in January 1776. He was then 38, and still an Ensign (2nd Lieutenant); this was usual for Rankers who could not pay for promotion and therefore had to wait for 'dead men's shoes'.

Two years earlier, 1782, a Royal Warrant had conferred County titles on all regiments not given special designations in addition to their numbers. The 24th was assigned to Warwickshire and was called '2nd Warwickshire' until 1881.

After a spell in Scotland the Regiment moved in 1785 again to Ireland, this time spending four undistinguished years there before embarking once more for Canada. They remained there, mainly in the backwoods, from 1789 to 1799. Up to this date, from Cornwallis' time, the Regiment had had two Colonels; William Taylor and Richard Whyte.

By this time the war with France was going badly, one
thorn in Britain's side being the French force which
Napoleon had left behind in Egypt in 1799, when his
grandiose plans to overrun the Middle East and capture
India came to nothing. This French army could not be
reinforced because of the ubiquitous British Navy; but it
was nonetheless in command of Egypt. It needed an expeditionary force to shift it, and when Sir Robert Abercromby essayed this task in 1801 the 24th and four other
battalions were sent out in June as reinforcements.

Their brigade at Alexandria consisted of themselves,
the 20th Foot, and the 'Ancient Irish Fencibles', who had
volunteered from the Irish Militia for service overseas.
The Commander was Brevet-Colonel Blake of the 24th,
leaving the effective control of the Regiment in the hands
of Lieutenant-Colonel Forster.

Abercromby died defeating the French outside Alexandria and his army, half the strength of the French, was
then commanded by General Hutchinson. The French
General Menou, despite the capitulation of the remaining
French forces, still held Alexandria, which was boxed in
by the British, who had flooded the dry bed of Lake
Mareotis and were using gunboats on it to bombard the
city. A force under General Coote reduced Fort Marabout
on the 21st of August, advancing from there up the narrow
isthmus to where the French waited, entrenched with
several field pieces on a ruin-covered ridge. The 24th (now
in Finches Brigade with the 26th and 54th) were part of
Coote's force. The skirmishers advanced warily on the
strongly held enemy position until the British gunboats on
Lake Mareotis opened up, completely enfilading the
French defences and causing a rapid withdrawal towards
Alexandria. The skirmishers succeeded in securing the
heavy guns, together with some prisoners, with very little
loss to themselves. This brought Coote within long bombardment range of the city. Siege guns were brought up;

in the intense heat the soldiers worked day and night until,
on the 26th of August, the reinforced batteries gave Alexandria such a pounding that Menou opened negotiations.
By this time the defenders were eating horsemeat; they
were so thin on the ground that they could not fully man
their outposts.

The defeated French were allowed to embark for their
own country; their expulsion from Egypt freed the Middle
East and India from the threat of Napoleon's imperialism.
Relief came on the 1st of November when the Regiment
left for Malta, where it stayed until returning to England
in March 1802 after the Peace of Amiens.

The Sphinx, superscribed Egypt, was ordered to be
borne on the colours 'as a distinguishing mark of His
Majesty's royal approbation and a lasting memorial of the
glory acquired by His Majesty's arms by the zeal, discipline and intrepidity of his troops in that arduous and
important campaign'. But it was not until a half-century
later, in June 1847, that a British War Medal (with the
clasp 'Egypt') was granted to all surviving ranks who
fought in Egypt. Only six officers and fifteen other ranks
claimed it.

CHAPTER SIX

1803–1814

THE FALSE SENSE of security brought by the Peace
of Amiens subsided as the ambitious Napoleon
gradually concentrated what was obviously an invasion force in the area around Boulogne and, when the
invasion of England seemed certain, Prime Minister Pitt
took action to strengthen the Army.

This resulted in the formation of a number of second
battalions, including one of the 24th. It came into being at
Warwick in September, 1804, (some forty-six years after
its forerunner became the progenitor of the 69th Foot) for
Home Service only.

But following the defeat of the Franco-Spanish fleet off
Trafalgar and the move of Napoleon's Grand Army to the
Danube the strategical situation changed; and when the
danger of invasion diminished the new second battalions
became available for active employment abroad. This
significant event opened the way for the 2/24th to future
fame under Wellington in the Peninsular War.

Meanwhile in August, 1805, the 1/24th, much below
strength, had sailed for South Africa as part of an expeditionary force under Sir David Baird. Now that the French
no longer directly threatened England's shores it was at
last possible to dispatch troops to wrest Cape Town from
Napoleon's allies, the Dutch.

The expedition found it difficult to land near Table
Bay and Baird dispatched Brigadier-General Beresford
with the 38th and the Light Dragoons to land some ninety

miles north of Cape Town, intending to follow on later if he could not force a landing nearer the Dutch stronghold. But the next day (the 6th of January, 1806) Baird was able to put the Highland Brigade ashore against light opposition; the 1/24th followed the next evening.

Realizing the value of quick action Baird pushed on the next morning without waiting for Beresford. A rough track took them across the Blaauberg Ridge, whose high ground, some 12 miles from Cape Town, the British force secured before the Dutch, under General Janssens, could take advantage of its dominating position. Janssens had left Cape Town early that morning with a force estimated by Baird at some 5,000 men and 20 guns. The Dutch were forced to deploy in the low ground below the ridge, and from their disposition Baird judged that Janssens' intention was to hold back on his (the Dutchman's) right and to try to turn the British flank on the seaward side of the ridge.

Baird sent his Highland Brigade forward along the track to attack Janssens' right wing while his other brigade (commanded in Beresford's absence by Baird's brother, the Lieutenant-Colonel of the 83rd) moved out towards the seaward side against the enemy's left. The 1/24th were in this latter brigade, with the 59th and 83rd, and to cover the British deployment Colonel Graham of the 93rd was pushed forward with a battalion made up from the British Light companies.

Graham quickly realized that the grenadiers of the 1/24th, who had gone off to occupy the 'heel of the Great Hill' running seawards across his front, were in trouble because a strong Dutch mounted contingent was riding in from Janssens' left to intercept them. Knowing that the heavily armed grenadiers were not good at skirmishing, Graham ordered the 1/24th Light Company out of cover over to the right to assist the grenadiers, who by this time had lost their commander (Captain Forster) and several men. Despite a sharp cannonade from two enemy guns and a hail of fire from his sharpshooters the 'Light Bobs' of the 1/24th, now closely supported by the other Light Companies increased their pressure until, to use Graham's quaint phraseology, the order to charge was given and 'how Mynheer did run, to be sure!'

The 1/24th, bearing the brunt of the fighting on the British right, had lost some 22 killed, missing and wounded, as against the 15 casualties of the other regiments. The Highland Brigade, facing stiffer opposition, kept up the momentum and soon, before the main body of the 1/24th were fully committed, the whole Dutch force broke in disorder; Baird's cavalry had not yet arrived and his exhausted infantry, short of water and conspicuous in the scrubby, sandy hinterland, were unable to press the pursuit.

But even so, Janssens had learned his lesson. He left the defence of Cape Town to a motley force of French sailors and Waldeck mercenaries whilst he withdrew to Hottentot's Holland, a mountain refuge away to the east of the settlement. On January the 10th, 1807, the British occupied Cape Town and eight days later the Dutch forces capitulated. The Cape was secured, British interests in Eastern waters were safe and now the 1/24th settled down to the humdrum life of garrison duty; there to stay for almost four years, isolated from the tumultuous events now taking place in Europe.

While the 1st Battalion was on active service at the Cape the 2nd Battalion remained in England as a draft-finding unit. During this time the Spaniards had risen against the French because of Napoleon's decision to put his brother Joseph on the throne of Spain. England, now free from the threat of invasion, seized this opportunity of striking a blow against the French and in 1808 Sir Arthur Wellesley, later the famous 'Iron Duke' of Wellington, landed in Portugal with the intention of driving the French Marshal Junot out of the country.

The 2/24th was not included in this expedition although Sir David Baird, who had been in command at the Cape (and who became Colonel of the Regiment in 1807), accompanied the ill-fated Sir John Moore on his abortive advance on Madrid and the famous retreat to Corruna in 1808. But when Wellesley went back to Portugal in April 1809 the 2/24th landed at Lisbon within a week of his arrival.

Wellesley's British Army at the commencement of the campaign was about 26,500 strong. He had a good solid corps of four divisions made up of 20 British Battalions and 4 of the King's German Legion; he also had 6 regiments of cavalry. Later he was to integrate Portuguese regiments with a hard core of British officers into his divisions while his Spanish allies, although good fighters under favourable conditions, were unreliable under pressure.

These same Spaniards were committed to supplying the Allied force with food and transport, but their widespread incompetence failed to meet the needs of the army, who were forced to live off the land.

On the 22nd July 1809 the 2/24th, part of Wellesley's main force, reached the outskirts of the village of Talavera. They mustered almost 800 all ranks and spent a miserable night with very little food because their baggage and rations had been plundered by Spanish fugitives, who had also stolen the Company books and money.

On the 28th of July Marshal Victor attacked at Talavera, outnumbering Wellesley two to one. The 2/24th, part of General Mackenzie's brigade with the 31st and 45th, were thrown in against the Nassau regiment, killing or wounding some 300 of them; then General Campbell's division promptly counter attacked, passing through Mackenzie's brigade and capturing some enemy guns. When Campbell paused to regroup at the Portina stream his example was followed by Brigadier Cameron, but the Guards and the Germans on the flanks of Cameron's brigade pushed on across the brook, only to be caught by the French second line and forced back in disorder, taking Cameron's men with them.

Mackenzie moved forward to stop the French attack; the 2/24th wheeled to allow the Guards through and then reformed their solid line, pouring volley after volley into the enemy while the Guards regrouped behind them. At this point Mackenzie was killed, but the 2/24th with the rest of his brigade kept up the pressure until, after half an hour's desperate fighting, the Guards again advanced. As the enemy wavered Cotton's Light Dragoons rode full tilt into the enemy's flank adding to a confusion which developed into a concerted attack by the British, and by five o'clock the battle was over.

This was one of the dourest battles in the war. The cost to Wellesley was 5,300 men, while the French lost more than 7,000. Forty-six per cent of the 2/24th became casualties (more than any other unit except a battalion of the King's German Legion) but this dear price purchased the first of the nine Battle Honours which the Regiment gained from the Peninsular War. Wellesley was made a Viscount and took the title of Viscount Wellington of Talavera.

Wellington, unable to exploit his success because of lack of help from the Spaniards, decided to retreat to Badajoz; it was not until September 1810 that he was able to strike back, at Busaco. Again the French were numerically superior. Marshal Massena was in command with Ney leading an army of 80,000 men, many of them veterans of Marengo and Austerlitz.

The 2/24th, now commanded by Major Chamberlain, were about 360 strong, but only their Light Company, merged with the skirmishers of General Spencer, was able to participate fully in the battle. In the fierce fighting that followed, the excellence of the British 'Sharp-shooters', at that time the finest marksmen in Europe, contributed to a disastrous defeat in which the French lost three times more men than Wellington. The Duke, who now had an opportunity of silencing his critics at home, was determined to prove that the French could be defeated in Portugal, but it was not until the following year that he was able to strike again decisively against the enemy.

By this time the British base at Lisbon was sending a steady stream of munitions and supplies to the army in the field. But the French, against whom the tide was turning,

Pte. Timothy Boot's medal showing the battles in which the 24th took part in the Peninsula.

adhered to their policy of living off a land which was depleted by lack of cultivation and ravaged by foul weather and hordes of refugees. These factors helped Wellington when he once more defeated Marshal Massena at the battle of Fuentes d'Onoro on 5th May 1811.

The 2/24th were among the weakest battalions in the First Division but their young soldiers of Talavera were now seasoned by two years of the Peninsula. Their first action in this battle came when they, with the 79th, supported the 71st in a counter-attack against General Ferey's Division, which they drove out of the village of Fuentes with very little loss to themselves. That was on the 3rd May, but it was two more days, with the 2/24th in a mainly supporting role, before the final British counter-attack ultimately forced Massena out of the savagely contested village.

Three days later the French were in full retreat. Wellington left the First Division, the 2/24th among them, as part of a holding force near Almeida, watching the movements of Marshal Marmont who had replaced Massena as the Commander of the French Army of Portugal.

The French system of living off the land caused their soldiers to disperse widely across the Portuguese countryside; Wellington turned this to account by besieging Ciudad Rodrigo, where the 2/24th did their stint of trench duty in bitter weather, losing some 20 men from a French sortie, but did not take part in the storming of the citadel on January the 19th, 1812. Because of this they did not get the battle honour of 'Ciudad Rodrigo' even though their part in the siege equalled that of some battalions who received the honour.

For some time after this there was hard marching but little fighting for the 2/24th. On more than one occasion Wellington almost caught Marmont with his forces dispersed, for the Duke wanted to bring him to battle before he could concentrate and when the French finally decided to attack, the British, for the first time in the campaign, found themselves outnumbering their enemies; the date was July 22nd, 1812, the place Salamanca.

A short but very sharp encounter followed, and in forty minutes Wellington had beaten 40,000 French while a large proportion of his army looked on, for the Duke did not use three of his available divisions. This policy of committing only those strictly necessary was typical of Wellington; on occasions he used single battalions to carry out specific tasks, as he did with the 2/24th at the siege of Burgos, some three months after Salamanca.

After an enforced rest because of heavy casualties, mainly from sickness, Wellington chose the First Division to reduce the French strong points, while the rest of the army regrouped at Madrid. At Burgos it took the Division two hectic weeks to clear the outer defences and fire a mine to breach the wall. But the storming parties, mixed British and Portuguese, were repulsed and Wellington decided to use a single battalion to force the breach. He chose the 2/24th.

Colonel Jones, the Engineer in charge, exploded the mine at 5 p.m. on the 4th of October. As he did so he was hit by a bullet, but the mine went off and about a hundred feet of rampart was demolished. Before the smoke had cleared the whole of the 2/24th, headed by Lieutenant Fraser, rushed the breach with such speed that they were covered in dust and showered with falling debris. They forced the gap and killed many French before Captain Lepper brought the covering party in to enlarge the breach. As this was going on Lieutenant Holmes was leading an assault across open ground on to the heavily defended second gap, swarming through it in the face of fierce resistance. Captain Coote backed him up with a second wave but was engaged and wounded by a French sergeant in single combat.

Captain Hedderwick, the senior officer left in the battalion, rallied the whole 2/24th in a sweeping bayonet charge which cut the defenders down and opened the way for the backing-up force to move into the breach. Only then did the small (there were only 198 rank and file), but gallant band pause to collect their wounded. They lay where they were until nightfall, when Wellington had them relieved.

This fierce foray had been witnessed by a huge concourse and Wellington himself was present at the time. It caught the imagination of the whole army and, despite the unsatisfactory end to the siege of Burgos, it brought the Regiment great renown. The spirited and audacious attack was pressed home so quickly that, comparatively speaking, the casualties were few; altogether twelve were killed and 58 wounded.

Wellington was never given to fulsome praise, but when in his dispatch, he described the 2/24th as 'highly praiseworthy' it was an accolade richly deserved.

During the rest of the campaign the Regiment, now veterans, marched from the flat and malarious plains of Portugal through Spain to the sacred soil of France, often covering 40 miles of rugged country at a stretch. Some of the fiercest engagements were concluded with hardly a shot being fired because, as the Welsh General Picton had remarked, the bayonet was the finest weapon of assault against the French: 'No powder,' he used to say, 'We'll do this work with the cold iron.'

Wellington was loath to dilute his veterans with replacements and the 2/24th had been linked with the 2/58th to form the 3rd Provisional Battalion, and transferred to the 7th Division which marched in Wellington's great enveloping movement to Vittoria where he completely defeated King Joseph's Army.

As Napoleon's men withdrew stubbornly across the

Pyrenees the British harried them enduring bitter weather and much sickness before the two important battles of Nivelle and Orthes brought the enemy to their knees.

In April 1814 the news of Napoleon's abdication brought the hard and bitter Peninsular war to its finish. At a cost of many brave men it ended a despot's rule and gave England another breathing space, during which, inevitably, the 2nd battalion was disbanded. It was lucky that the 24th had been represented by a 2nd Battalion which had fought so well in the greatest series of campaigns fought by the British Army. Talavera was its greatest day.

On 24th November all that remained of this magnificent fighting machine were some 300 'old sweats', who still had a part to play as a Depot and training cadre for the 1st Battalion. That they fulfilled their purpose cannot be disputed, as the Regiment's record in India will show.

CHAPTER SEVEN

1810–1849

IN 1810 THE 1st Battalion's pleasant sojourn in South Africa ended. On June the 10th, almost eleven hundred strong, they embarked in five 'East Indiamen' for service in India; but accident and delay held up two of the ships shortly after the start. The remaining three ships sailed on uneventfully until July the 3rd, when they were intercepted off Madagascar by three French men-of-war, who immediately attacked and scattered the small fleet.

The *Astell*, carrying about 300 of the 1/24th, though badly damaged and shipping water, made a run for it and reached Madras on the 1st of August. The two ships left behind at the Cape also turned up in India some months later, and by the end of November there were 25 officers and 659 N.C.O.s and men of the Regiment in Calcutta.

The others were taken prisoner in the two Indiamen, *Ceylon* and *Windham*, and sailed to French-held Mauritius where they were given a friendly reception by the enemy garrison. Before the French boarded the *Ceylon* Colonel Marriott had the Colours and the regimental records thrown overboard (an act lamented many years later by the Regimental Historian, Professor Atkinson). After a while the French put pressure on the prisoners, persuading about 20 of them to desert the British Service and join the enemy. When, in November, a British expedition captured Mauritius eleven of these turncoats were captured and, surprisingly in those harsh days, were allowed to go free when they agreed to serve permanently in the East with the forces of 'John Company'.

In March 1811 the 1st Battalion was finally reunited at Fort William, near Calcutta, remaining there until the troubles with the Kingdom of Nepaul caused them to move north in July 1814 to Dinapur, on a tributary of the Ganges. Soon the Governor-General, Lord Moira, decided to use force against the Gurkhas and the 1/24th became a part of the Eastern column of General Marley's 17,000 strong army, bound for Khatmandu via the Bhagmati valley, then an area of steep, unexplored, thickly-forested country.

The incidents which followed provide an illuminating sidelight on the varied abilities of the senior officers of that day. General Marley was in the employ of the East India Company, and has been described as being 'without energy or enterprise'. He clearly disliked the idea of attacking the Gurkhas and, although he had 8,000 men in his column, it took him the whole of December to move the main body some fifty miles from his advanced depot at Bettiah to the edge of the forest belt.

On January the 1st, 1815, the Gurkhas successfully attacked two of his isolated outposts, whereupon he hastily decamped to Bettiah, dug himself in, and declared that his force was too weak to take the offensive. This brought a severe rebuke from Lord Moira, himself a proven soldier of the American campaigns; his charge of 'mischievous indecision' caused Marley to quit his camp forthwith, leaving no word, nor appointing a deputy. General E. Wood, who relieved Marley, did little better. The 1/24th, who during these curious happenings had been split into two parts, each operating with native battalions, must have been glad when the rains broke and they moved back to camp near Bettiah.

There they remained, the sick-rate steadily mounting, until October. It was not until February 1816, in a column commanded by its own Lieutenant-Colonel, Kelly, that the battalion took part in a new campaign under

General Ochterlony which achieved a measure of success against the Gurkhas, who sustained heavy casualties and were forced to ask for terms. On March the 6th peace was signed and the 1/24th came back to base to find a General Order from Lord Moira commending Colonel Kelly on 'the able and gallant manner in which he had achieved the arduous task assigned to him'.

It took the battalion two weeks to march back to Dinapur, where, with hardly time to re-equip, the Flank Companies left on a punitive expedition against the Pindaris and their Mahratta supporters. In October 1817 the remaining companies left Dinapur to assist in guarding the Bengal border but never came into action and, five months later, the whole battalion moved back to its old station.

While still at Dinapur it was learned that in August 1817 the Prince Regent had authorized the Regiment to bear the Battle Honours 'Talavera', 'Fuentes D'Onor', 'Pyrenees' and 'Orthes' on its Colours; these now joined 'Egypt' in the growing list of honours. Several more years were spent in moving from garrison to garrison and then, seventeen years after leaving home, the battalion prepared to embark for England. Its twelve years in India had not brought many opportunities of greatness, though it had held its own in difficult country, often under severe conditions. But the next tour in the sub-continent was to be very different.

The battalion landed in England in July 1823, moving from Portsmouth to Devonport in search of recruits. The inevitable sojourn in Ireland came in September 1825, but before leaving England the Regiment received new Colours (21st March, 1825), on which the additional battle-honours of 'Salamanca', 'Vittoria', 'Nivelle' and 'Peninsula' were borne. The tour in Ireland lasted four years, then the battalion moved to Lancashire, where it was soon preparing for its third trip to North America.

The battalion travelled the first stage of its journey to Canada by canal boat, leaving Manchester on the 23rd of July 1829 and arriving at Paddington four days later. The voyage across the Atlantic took a tedious nine weeks, and while the Regiment was at sea its Colonel, Sir David Baird, died. He was replaced by Major-General Sir James Lyon, whose only contact with the 24th was as an Inspecting Officer in 1823.

The political situation in Canada when the Regiment arrived was not unlike that of today. French Canadians in Lower Canada were pressing for a republic and the place 'teemed with disaffection', but seven years were to pass before the trouble broke. Desertion was unusually heavy and in the years 1836 and 1837 the battalion lost 110 men in this way. A draft of 111 arriving on July the 28th, 1837, barely redressed the balance.

Towards the end of 1837 an ugly situation had developed. Insurgents were openly training in the valley of the River Richelieu (which the battalion had traversed in 1776) and when some of them clashed with Government forces Sir John Colborne, Commander-in-Chief in Canada, decided to act. The Flank companies of the battalion formed part of a force of 300 under Colonel Gore. They were sent downstream from Sorel to disperse a party of insurgents gathered at the village of St. Denis, starting their 26-mile march on a night of freezing rain clad in full winter kit.

Gore drove his men on relentlessly but when they arrived, exhausted and half-frozen, he found the rebels in strongly manned stone buildings too well-defended for one light gun and a handful of weary men. After three hours' hard fighting in which he incurred twenty casualties (10 of them 24th men), Gore left his gun frozen in the mud and trudged back to Sorel.

A week later he went back again with a stronger force, including the light company of the 24th, but the birds had flown and the best that he could do was to destroy the buildings that had held him up, and recover his solitary gun. After that Gore tramped the surrounding country to assert the Royal authority, returning to Montreal on December the 11th, 1837.

The battalion operated from Montreal over the next few years, sending a company here and a detachment there as the need arose. They took part in the suppression of the 1838 rebellion, which started with the proclamation of a Canadian Republic at Napierville, near the American border, but soon after this the trouble died down. When, in June 1841, the battalion was ordered home, it left almost 200 men behind as voluntary reinforcements for other regiments in Canada. The G.O.C., General Jackson, wrote them a farewell letter in which he said that he could not 'let you go without a line to say how well satisfied I have been in every respect with the 24th Regiment since I have been in Canada. No Regiment here is more entitled to commendation'.

The 24th had no share in the first Sikh War of 1845–46. They arrived in India between August and September in 1846, after a five-year stay in the United Kingdom, to find the Sikh power unbroken and its leaders chafing under the terms imposed upon them. Within two years of the battalion's arrival an incident at Multan, which resulted in the murder of two British officers, sparked off the second Sikh War. On 3rd of October 1848 the 24th, now over 1,000 strong, marched north to join General Sir Hugh Gough's 'Army of the Punjaub' at Ferozepore. Field-Marshal Norman saw 'this splendid-looking Corps' on the 350-mile march and wrote: 'I never before or since have seen companies fall in so strong. . . . They were smart and composed of fine men'. They were to need their strength in the grim campaign to come.

Gough's plan was to bring the Sikh leader, Shere Singh,

to battle without delay, but when he got to the Chenab River he found the enemy well installed, and particularly strong in artillery. He spent a frustrating fortnight trying to lure the enemy out on to the open plain, then decided to send a column under General Thackwell to ford the river some twelve miles up, thus turning the Sikh flank. The force left at midnight on 1st December, leaving its tents standing and fires burning; but they found the fording area impassable and had to trudge a further ten miles up the river to Wazirabad, where the 24th crossed to the far side and held it until the main body crossed.

Thackwell pushed quickly down the right bank without opposition until he reached Sadullapur, where the enemy were drawn up in fields of thick sugar cane, an ideal obstacle against the British, who had outpaced their guns. Thackwell used subterfuge to try and get the Sikhs into the open; the 24th were ordered into a mock retirement of several hundred yards but the enemy merely intensified his artillery fire, causing heavy casualties among the British.

That night was cold and unpleasant for the 24th and their comrades. Rations were scarce and the officers dined on cold tea and chuppatis. The Sikhs unwittingly helped the famished 24th by shooting Major Harris's horse from under him; this unexpected gift was quickly turned into soup and steaks by the starving soldiers, some of whom had not eaten a hot meal for three days. That night the enemy slipped away unseen; they went north to the River Jhelum where, because the Governor-General vetoed Gough's follow-up (and partly because supplies were short), the Sikhs gained more than a month to prepare an exceptionally strong defensive position.

When General Gough finally resumed his advance he found Shere Singh, with 30,000 Sikhs, holding a six-mile front on the left bank of the river. The enemy regular troops manned the right, strongly supported by fanatical irregulars occupying almost inaccessible, ravine-crossed ground on the left. Gough, having only 13,000 men and knowing the enemy to be well-endowed with guns, decided on caution. On the 13th of January, 1849, he occupied the village of Chillianwala against Sikh skirmishers, looking for a place to deploy, because, remembering Shere Singh's stratagem on the Chenab, he did not foresee an immediate battle. Arms were piled and guns were parked, the cavalry unsaddled their horses; then, for want of something better to do, Lieutenant Macpherson climbed a handy tree to view the jungle front.

His shout of alarm must have petrified those below. Advancing towards them through the thick, tangled undergrowth he saw waves of turbaned Sikh heads. Simultaneously the enemy opened up with heavy and accurate artillery fire from the guns that Shere Singh had secretly brought forward. Later some said that this enemy attack was premature; it certainly achieved complete surprise, and Gough was caught quite unprepared. Bugles sounded 'Stand to', and as the troops frantically grabbed their weapons and took up offensive positions (for retreat never crossed Gough's mind) a general attacking movement developed along the whole hastily-formed British line.

Then an incident, which Gough later described as 'an act of madness', took place. The 24th, advancing in the centre of Pennycuick's brigade, heard Sir Colin Campbell, commander of the 2nd Division, who was moving up with Hoggan's brigade on their left, shout, 'Do not load, this work is to be done with the bayonet'; (a not unusual order, for Gough himself had earlier stressed the importance of the bayonet, telling the 24th to 'give them the cold steel, my boys'.) It was in the spirit of the Peninsula, but in this jungle setting its consequences were tragic, and Gough afterwards conceded that it would have been better 'to put in a volley or two before storming the guns'.

The British advance started at 3 p.m. Through thick impenetrable scrub the 24th marched in the centre, their Grenadier Company skirmishing ahead, desperately trying to keep some sort of line as the harassing Sikh artillery fire took its toll. The enemy positions were unknown to the soldiers, the thick undergrowth concealed all without giving the least protection. After the first two hundred yards all semblance of a line vanished. One can imagine the private soldiers' mute, questioning glance, 'How far, Corporal?' The corporal does not know, neither does the General for that matter; it is a question of getting to the Sikh guns before the terrible cannonade cuts them down.

The pace instinctively increased until it became a mad rush. Pennycuick was in the vanguard but there was no real control; as he encouraged the 24th onward he noticed that the Indian Sepoys on the flanks were being left behind. The trees thinned out a little and the soldiers rushed into the clearings, thinking that they were at the jungle edge, only to be mown down by the Sikh gunfire. No one seems to have given a formal order to charge (indeed, after an investigation later, Sir Charles Napier stated that no such order had been given), in the danger and excitement there was a spontaneous rush to get at the enemy with the only weapon that could be used, the bayonet. A survivor's account sums it up: 'The Regiment never wavered in the face of the artillery fire, it pressed on without firing a shot. Grape, canister and roundshot mowed them down by the score; and how did they answer? By a rousing cheer.'

What men they were! Lieutenant Macpherson of the 24th wrote: 'My company was near the centre, we held the Colours and made a good target. One charge of grapeshot took away an entire section and for a moment I was alone and unhurt. On we went, the goal is almost won, the ground clears, the pace quickens . . .' (they could now see the flashes of those lethal guns, the Sikh soldiers labouring at the heavy shells) '. . . the bayonets came down to the charge. My men's pieces were loaded but not a shot was fired, with a wild, choking Hurrah we stormed the guns and the battery is won.'

Sir Colin Campbell was emphatic in his praise: 'It is impossible for any troops to have surpassed the gallantry of this attack. This single Regiment actually broke the enemy's line and took the large number of guns to their front.'

General Napier was also impressed: 'Their conduct,' he declared, 'has never been surpassed by British soldiers on a field of battle.' And all this without firing a single shot. The Grenadier Company were first to the guns; they were counter-attacked and driven back but rallied under Captain Travers and surged forward again, this time backed up by the rest of the 24th.

The Sikhs fought bravely and fanatically, even firing on their own soldiers in their effort to save the cannon stormed by the 24th; but they failed. A small force led by Lieutenant Lutman and Sergeant Lear spiked the guns. Again and again the enemy counter-attacked until the centre company of the 24th was almost annihilated. The remnants, to quote Napier, stood their ground 'alone in their glory'. The entire Colour Party was shot down, both officers (Lieutenant Phillips and Ensign Collins) were killed virtually on the muzzles of the guns. Colonel Penny-cuick was killed too, dying inside the enemy position, while his son, newly joined from Sandhurst, was shot down vainly trying to save him.

The 24th desperately bayonetted the remaining Sikhs, striving to stem the stream of enemy reinforcements. But the terrible casualties in the centre had opened up a gap which the lagging Indian Army Sepoys failed to fill. Shere Singh's men broke through this weak spot, swarming around the rear of the battalion and forcing them back. As they retired they met the Sepoys coming up and the

Chilianwala, January 13th, 1849. Junior Ensign Pennycuick, just out from Sandhurst, guards the body of his dead father, Colonel Pennycuick. He himself was killed almost at once.

Indian soldiers, perhaps thinking that the retreat was general, also fell back. But as soon as open ground was reached the 24th rallied.

By this time Captain Blachford was the senior officer left. Conspicuous by his bravery he reformed the ranks, rallying first number 7 Company, and then stragglers from other Companies mustered by Lieutenant Barry, who was hit, but staggered on as the surviving subalterns rushed to their comrades' side. Many walking wounded joined in the new attack which, weak though it was, gave the other brigade (Hoggan's) a breathing space and allowed the British guns to be brought up (at this time, the Sikh fire was concentrated on the small pocket of 24th survivors and this allowed the main British counter-attack to be launched).

The attack was led by Colin Campbell in person, building on the successes of the 24th and forcing the enemy to retire. True to its traditions, the remnants of the Regiment reformed and joined in the final attack against the retreating Sikhs. Then, first into action and last out, they helped to bring in some of the captured guns though after dark the Sikhs contrived to take away most of the remaining pieces.

Sundown brought a night of torment. Torrential rain poured down as the wounded, almost three hundred of them belonging to the 24th, waited without food or drink for the search parties to find them. One account speaks of the dead of the Regiment lying in lines so that 'in some places you would think the men had had the word to lie down'. In two trenches alone were buried 197 men of the 24th with 14 of the 61st; of the 31 officers and 1,065 soldiers who went in to the attack 13 officers and 225 were killed and 9 officers and 278 wounded. The most miraculous happening of the battle was surely the survival of Lieutenant Lloyd Williams, who, after being 'knocked out' near the guns, became a target for stabbing, slicing

Sikh horsemen until at their retreat he had sustained twenty-three lance and sword wounds, a fractured skull, and the loss of his left hand. But, indestructible Welshman that he was, he recovered to retire as a Captain in 1851, living on for almost forty years. The Queen's Colour vanished in the fighting, some spoke of seeing it wrapped about the body of Private Connelly, who had taken it from the broken pike just before he was killed. It may be that the Colour was buried with him. The Sikhs say they never saw it, although they proudly displayed the captured Colours of the 25th B.N.I. and 45th Native Infantry Regiments. The Regimental Colour was rescued by Private Perry, who was promoted corporal on the field, and on discharge received the Good Conduct medal and an annuity of £20. This Colour now hangs, with the tattered remnants of others equally illustrious, in the Regimental Chapel at Brecon Cathedral, which has become the hallowed last resting place of all Colours presented to the Regiment since 1812 (excepting those irretrievably lost).

Professor Atkinson calls Gough's action at Chillianwala a Pyrrhic victory, for although Shere Singh lost many men before he moved away to Gujerat he had weakened the British force to such an extent that Gough could not exploit his success. But for the 24th the battle was a victory of the first magnitude; a victory of guts and cold steel over unfavourable conditions and overwhelming odds which will never be forgotten.

On February the 21st, 1849, Gough's reinforced army once more met Shere Singh's men, at Gujerat. The 24th were still in Campbell's Division, serving with the 25th N.I. Regiment in Carnegy's brigade, which faced the Sikh army across the dry bed of the Dwara river.

Gough was not to be caught by the Sikh guns this time. He bombarded Shere Singh's batteries for three hours, reducing them to virtual silence before the British infantry advanced. The 24th, on Campbell's right, had two companies out in front as skirmishers, while the main body was well sheltered from enemy fire in a dry nullah. Several spirited charges by the Sikh cavalry were repelled with heavy losses, and when the British attack was pressed home the enemy broke and ran. The end was in sight; the Sikh leader surrendered at Rawalpindi on March the 14th, 1849. Although the 24th bore their fair share in the engagement, and had been for some time under bombardment, as if by a special act of Providence not a man was lost. The Regiment moved to Wazirabad but eight months elapsed before a permanent camp was provided so that the married men who survived could be joined by their families.

CHAPTER EIGHT

1850–1879

THE THIRD 2ND BATTALION in the Regiment's history was formed at Sheffield on the 3rd of June 1858 and, for the first time, the Army List distinguishes between Officers of the two battalions, putting a '1' or '2' against their names. There were twenty-five of these battalions raised to the Line Regiments (from the 2nd of Foot to the 25th, plus the Rifle Brigade) and the fierce competition for recruits left most of them, including the 2/24th, below strength for some time.

Under Lieutenant-Colonel Sir Charles Ellice (not to be confused with General Robert Ellice, who was Colonel of the Regiment from 1842 to 1856) the newly-fledged battalion was presented with Colours by Lady Wharncliffe a month before it moved to Aldershot; which had just been established as a military cantonment.

However, for the 2/24th the stay at Aldershot was short. An 'unfortunate affray' with some men of a Militia battalion, who cast aspersions on the Regiment's officers, resulted in a personal 'telling-off' from the Duke of Cambridge, who was then Commander-in-Chief: 'If I had my way,' the Duke told them, 'I'd send you all to—well a place not mentioned in the Queen's Regulations, but as I can't send you there you'll go to Mauritius for a spell.' And in March 1860 off to Mauritius they went, leaving two depot companies behind to find recruits.

They stayed there for six pleasant years, presumably not quite what Cambridge intended, then went on to Burma, where in the autumn of 1865 they were stationed at Rangoon. One of their duties was to find a contingent of 3 officers and 100 men for duty in the Andaman Islands, where in May 1867 reports that the crew of a British ship had been murdered by the hostile natives of Little Andaman were investigated by a party from the 2/24th detachment. When they arrived at the scene of the reputed massacre, a landing in two small craft was attempted despite the heavy surf and a hail of arrows from the aggressive natives.

One boat's crew managed to wade ashore through the turbulent water and soon discovered what they took to be a European skull on the shore. By now their ammunition was almost exhausted and to prevent them being overrun they were recalled to the ship. As the shore party tried to re-embark from the rock their boat capsized, forcing them to move back to the original landing place, finding the partially buried bodies of four more Europeans on the way.

Strenuous efforts were made to get to the shore party through the tumbling surf, both by boat and raft, during which the party's leader, Lieutenant Much, was washed overboard and almost drowned. When all else had failed Assistant-Surgeon Douglas and four men, Privates Bell, Cooper, Griffiths and Murphy, volunteered to man a gig and try again. In the high-running seas the soldiers, under the determined leadership of Douglas, handled the boat with coolness and determination; shuttling through the heavy surf in constant danger of being swamped, until the whole party had been ferried back to the ship and were 'thus rescued from the virtual certainty of being massacred and eaten by the savages'.

When the incident was reported to the Commander-in-Chief in India he recommended that all five should receive the Victoria Cross. This was the first award of the coveted decoration to the Regiment, though it must be remembered that at this time (while the gallantry and courage of the men concerned, in the face of the Queen's enemies, was of a very high order) the carefully selective procedures which now govern the award of the Victoria Cross had not yet been introduced.

The excellent sporting facilities enjoyed in Burma were renewed when the 2/24th moved to India in December 1868. Apart from game-bird shooting, such exotic pas-times as mounted panther-sticking and tiger hunting took up much of the officers' time, as well as the more mundane pursuits of hunting jackals and foxes.

In the autumn of the following year two 2/24th officers distinguished themselves by their bravery, both being volunteers attached to Sir Garnett Wolseley's expedition to Coomassie. Captain C. J. Bromhead was mentioned in dispatches and received a Brevet-Majority (he was the brother of Gonville, who was later awarded the Victoria Cross after Rorke's Drift) and Lieutenant Lord Gifford, who became the Regiment's sixth V.C., for conspicuous skill and gallantry while commanding native Scouts.

Thirteen years after their 'banishment' by the Duke of Cambridge the 2nd Battalion returned to England, sailing home through the recently opened Suez Canal to Ports-mouth, where they landed in January 1873. In the April of that year their depot companies, with those of the 1st Battalion, were consolidated at Brecon in South Wales, where the brigade depot (changing its name to 'Regimen-tal Depot' later) was to remain for eighty-seven years, almost to the day.

When the 2/24th was being formed in 1858 the 1st Battalion had still three years to serve in India. They had stayed on at Wazirabad after the Sikh surrender, enduring great heat and suffering from the prevalent enteric and ophthalmia. The 1/24th moved in December 1852 to Sialkot where they received news that the battle-honours 'Punjaub', 'Chilianwala' and 'Goojerat' had been awarded to the Regiment. Their next move was to Peshawar where they had their first experience of the Frontier tribesmen they were later to encounter in 1937. While here the Regiment was re-armed with the Enfield rifle in place of the old smooth bore.

When the Mutiny broke the 1st Battalion did not come into the centre of that great crisis but saw active employment and sharp fighting for all that, particularly when Lieutenant-Colonel Ellice with numbers 1, 2 and 3 Companies and three Horse Artillery guns were diverted to Jhelum, where the 14th and 39th Bengal Native Infantry were on the point of mutiny. The C.O. of the 14th, Colonel Gerrard, had ordered his men to give up their arms on the promise that the regiment would not be broken up (as other Bengal units were being), if they remained loyal. He was answered with a volley of fire and took refuge, with his officers, among Ellice's approaching column.

Colonel Ellice, with barely 300 of the 1/24th and three light guns, now faced a thousand well-armed mutineers fully prepared to kill all white men who came within their range. He attacked at once, taking the Sepoy's lines from the flank and chasing the mutineers from hut to hut, inflicting heavy casualties. Many of them took to their heels, but a hard core barricaded themselves in the stoutly built guard-house. The guns failed to silence their fire and the Colonel himself, mounted on a charger, led an attack up to the guard-room door where his horse was shot from under him and he received dangerous wounds in the neck and leg.

The British soldiers stormed on to take the guard-room; then turned against the lines of the 39th Native Infantry, where a fortunate shot from one of the guns blew up the magazine. The startled Sepoys took refuge in a walled village which Colonel Gerrard, who had taken over when Ellice was wounded, attacked as soon as his men had had some respite from the blazing sun. At 4 p.m.

the 1/24th advanced in skirmishing order, covered by the guns. Captain Spring was mortally wounded and two other officers badly hit, but despite this the attack was strongly pressed up to assaulting distance, when the supporting guns ran out of ammunition, and the British had to check.

It was decided to postpone operations until the morning, when reserve ammunition would be available, and the men spent the night bivouacked under arms close to the stockade. The next morning found the mutineers clear of the village, looking for better cover. They were pursued with vigour but the battalion lost heavily while mopping up; total casualities showed that one in every four had been hit, 24 being killed and 49 wounded, not including the officers lost the day before.

For many weeks the 1/24th found detachments and reinforced mobile columns to help preserve order. In addition to the battle casualties 25 men died of cholera at Amritsar and others died of heat exhaustion and sickness brought on by the vile conditions. It was with no regret that the battalion embarked for home at Karachi in March 1861.

The battalion landed, yet again, at Portsmouth. During its fifteen month stay in that area General Finch died and was succeeded as Colonel of the Regiment on the 26th of November 1861 by Major-General Pringle Taylor, an officer of the 22nd Light Dragoons who had distinguished himself in the Mahratta Wars. He was the last Colonel to come from outside the Regiment and one of the longest serving (twenty-three years).

In the next decade the 1st Battalion moved from England to Malta (after the inevitable tour in Ireland) and then to Gibraltar, where they spent three uneventful years. But these years wrought radical changes in the structure of the Army.

The Cardwell system of reforms was introduced, by which

Examples of the uniform and equipment worn by men of the 24th prior to departure for the South African war. Note the pioneers with their axes and the corporal fourth from the left who appears to be smoking a cigarette!

the number of infantry battalions at home and overseas 'balanced' each other for recruiting and draft-finding purposes, and short-term service (7 years with the Colours and 5 on reserve) came in. Military districts and sub-districts (each holding a 'brigade depot') were established throughout Britain so that recruit training assumed some degree of permanence and continuity. The groundwork for the assumption of the title 'The South Wales Borderers' was thus laid, but the change was not to come for another eight years.

On March the 9th, 1878, with the arrival of the 2/24th in South Africa, the two battalions of the Regiment for the first time operated in the same country and under the same command. The 1st Battalion had already been overseas for three years, campaigning under General Cunynghame against the Kaffirs in the Transkei, a land of wild, brush-covered veldt, criss-crossed with deep 'kloofs' and ravines. The 1/24th had raised and successfully used its first troops of Mounted Infantry (M.I.) in aid of the civil power against the European malcontents in the Diamond Field country around Kimberley; and afterwards against the Gaika and Galeka tribes at Quintana, crushing the rebellion raised by the Kaffir Chiefs.

These wide ranging operations over rough, open country had left the Regiment in a 'high state of drill and discipline' and when General Cunynghame handed over command to General Thesiger, later Lord Chelmsford, he issued an Order which said of the 24th. 'They have never failed to assist me, each and every duty that I have placed before them they have readily accepted and cheerfully accomplished, their excellence as marksmen bearing testimony to their good training.' These were the men who were to move north, mostly to their death, within a few short months.

The trouble of the Transkei tribes had been a pinprick compared to the menace now looming on the borders of Natal. There the Zulus, moulded into a mighty martial nation (by native standards), stood in contempt of the Boers and in open defiance of the British. Since 1815, when King Chaka had taken the boys from their mothers to train them on classical Spartan lines, the allegiance of the warrior was to the King and the Regiment, not to the tribe or the family.

Formed into groups called 'Impi's' they were forbidden marriage until their spears had been blooded in battle. Using their superb sense of concealment they could merge into the country as the lion used the long grass; they were lightly armed and could cover long distances at great speed, outrunning a horse over short stretches. Their greatest asset was the tactical use of their famous Crescent formation, which had a massed, solid centre from which two 'horns' grew out to encircle and engulf the enemy.

Behind the centre came the 'loins', line upon line of reinforcements, whose role was to fill the gaps in the forward ranks and to provide extra weight in the final assault.

Their present King, Cetewayo, had agreed to submit to British arbitration his long-standing quarrel with the Boers over the boundary between Zululand and the Transvaal. But when the High Commissioner (Sir Bartle Frere) announced in December 1878 that, among other conditions, Cetewayo must disband his army, allow his celibate soldiers to marry, and accept a British Resident into his Kingdom, he showed no sign of acceptance and relations between the Zulus and the British rapidly worsened.

Then some of Cetewayo's men mounted a raid into tribal territory in Natal, ostensibly to bring back runaway Zulu wives who had crossed the border. The British demanded that the raiders be handed over, and when Cetewayo refused, the Government, which had troops to spare now that the Kaffir War was over, gave the Zulu leader an ultimatum which expired on the 11th of January, 1879.

When no reply came, the British field-force had moved up to Rorke's Drift on the Buffalo river, later marching on Ulundi, the Zulu capital, leaving a small force to guard the base hospital. Lord Chelmsford had been appointed Commander-in-Chief. His force was organized into four columns, of which No. 3, commanded by Colonel Glyn late of the 24th, was the strongest; it included both the 1st and 2nd Battalions (less detached companies) as well as a field battery, a Mounted Infantry squadron and a native contingent some 2,600 strong (mainly from Natal).

Chelmsford decided to attach himself and his Staff to No. 3 Column, carefully pointing out to Colonel Glyn that he did not wish to interfere in his command or to 'accept responsibility for the numerous details which necessarily have to be considered by an officer commanding a column in the field'. This Colonel Glyn unreservedly accepted, although it was agreed that Chelmsford would be entirely responsible for the general direction of the Column, including reconnaissance, and would make all principal tactical decisions. Whether this demarcation was clear enough, and what complications Chelmsford caused by going with No. 3 Column is a matter for conjecture; many books and articles have discussed it at great length and it would be better here to concentrate on known events rather than to speculate.

The field-force, with No. 3 Column in the centre, moved on, leaving a reserve column under Colonel Durnford, R.E., to follow. 'I shall make sure,' said Lord Chelmsford to Durnford before they left, 'that as we advance we will not leave any large force of Zulus in our rear.' This was in accordance with his plan to drive the enemy before him and to destroy them at Ulundi. From this point on the story is concerned almost exclusively with No. 3 Column, which against light opposition camped on the 20th of January, 1879, under the huge, eroded rock that towered some 500 feet above the undulating slopes of Isandhlwana.

To the north the camp was dominated by high ground, though the other three sides could have been prepared for defence if proper entrenchments had been made according to the Field Manual then in use; however, this was not done. Colonel Glyn suggested building a 'laager' but was over-ruled because of the wagon shortage, perhaps it was thought that the Zulus dared not attack a force of 4,000 men.

Chelmsford probed the scrub-covered plains and dried stream beds towards the east, but when mounted vedettes reported enemy in strength to the north-east he decided instead to reconnoitre the south-east, sending Major Dartnell of the Natal Native Contingent (N.N.C.) with his levies and some mounted troops. They soon encountered a party of Zulus, from whom they captured several head of cattle; then Dartnell, smelling action, asked for permission to bivouac where he was, later sending for two companies of the 24th to come out to assist him in attacking the enemy.

Chelmsford refused to do this; he made his own decision. Rightly or wrongly he decided to take a much larger force and to accompany it himself. Assuming (so many authorities hold) that Dartnell had found the Zulu main body, Chelmsford left camp at 4 a.m. accompanied by Colonel Glyn and the 2/24th (less two companies) with four guns, and most of the mounted men available. They headed south-east, looking for the 'celibate, man-destroying gladiators' of Cetewayo.

CHAPTER NINE

1879
(21st/22nd January)

'The terrible disaster that overwhelmed the old 24th
Regiment will always be remembered, not so much as a
disaster, but as an example of heroism like that of Leonidas
and the three hundred Spartans who fell at the pass of
Thermopylae.'

> General Sir Reginald Hart, V.C.
> (At the unveiling of the
> Isandhlwana Memorial in March 1914)

A LONE OFFICER riding a tired horse over the open
veldt approached the gaunt, Sphinx-shaped rock
overlooking the British encampment at Isandhlwana. Weary and weak from lack of food he was riding
into the base to seek tents and rations for his native
soldiers. The officer was Commandant Lonsdale of the
1/3rd Natal Native Contingent, the date the 22nd of
January, 1879. He rode on into the lines of tents and was
suddenly confronted with a huge Zulu, covered in blood
and wearing a red tunic. Realizing that the camp had been
over-run and was at that moment being looted by the
Zulus, Lonsdale turned, spurred his tired horse through
the bullets and assegais and, miraculously, got clear to
break the news.

A Major Gossett was dispatched at once to Lord
Chelmsford's new camp, arriving there at about 4 p.m.
Chelmsford had already received a message from Colonel
Pulleine, the 24th Officer left in charge at Isandhlwana,

timed at 8.5 a.m. that morning and reporting that the Zulus were approaching his camp in some force from the north-east. Chelmsford merely remarked, 'There is nothing to be done on that', but later sent his A.D.C. and Captain Penn Symons, of the 24th, to check on the camp by telescope. It was some ten miles away but could be seen clearly and appeared quiet. Then, at 1.30 p.m., a second message came from Commandant Browne, who had already sighted Zulus in force after leaving Chelmsford's party to go back towards Isandhlwana with his battalion of N.N.C. 'For God's sake come with your men,' it said, 'the camp is surrounded.'

This alarming message had caused Major Harness, an Artillery officer, to start with an escort for Isandhlwana because, apart from the messages, gunfire had been heard from that direction at about 12.30 p.m. Harness was recalled, however, because Chelmsford, on getting Commandant Browne's second message had climbed a nearby hill and from it could see no sign of trouble at the camp. Other messages are said to have been dispatched but the facts are obscure; however, when Lord Chelmsford got Lonsdale's story from Major Gossett he rode at once for Isandhlwana, followed 30 minutes later by the 2/24th and the guns. The men marched nine miles in about two hours, catching up with Chelmsford's party when they halted temporarily some two miles from the camp. He addressed the soldiers briefly, with tears in his eyes: '24th, whilst we have been out yonder the enemy has outflanked us and taken our camp, they are probably holding it now; at any cost we must take it back tonight and cut our way back to Rorke's Drift tomorrow. This means fighting, but I know I can rely on you.'

The men cheered at this, then refilled their waterbottles and hurriedly marched on. And soon as they plunged onward, they could see, against the dying sun, parties of Zulus leaving Isandhlwana, driving wagons and herds of cattle before them. Darkness had fallen as they reached the camp; bayonets were fixed and the line of soldiers plunged forward into the darkness. 'All was as still as death,' Penn Symons afterwards wrote. 'It was a most trying time for our young soldiers; indeed, for all of us. Every instant we expected to be attacked. As we neared the camp we stumbled constantly over the naked, gashed and ghastly bodies of our comrades.' A few volleys were fired into the tents but there was no retaliation; then, sick with horror, the tired soldiers lay down to wait for dawn.

With first light came the shocking realization that almost the entire force had been butchered; in groups of 30 to 60 the defenders lay where they had been cut down, young boys and grizzled veterans, side by side and back to back. Loose and broken wagon wheels were scattered about, and around these, for some savage and macabre reason, the Zulus had placed circles of soldiers' severed heads.

What happened at Isandhlwana after Lord Chelmsford left to reinforce Dartnell? We know that before he left he ordered the reserve column commander, Colonel Durnford, to move up to the camp with his force of four companies of N.N.C., 250 mounted Basutos and a rocket battery manned by soldiers of the 24th. Had Durnford decided to remain in the camp he could have taken over its command because he was senior to Colonel Pulleine, but he showed no intention of staying and asked the latter for two companies of the 24th to strengthen his own force, adding that he would take the responsibility on himself.

As Pulleine had less than 1,500 men to defend the camp (426 of them were 1/24th with about 171 of the 2/24th; 60 men of the R.A. with two guns; about 800 of the Natal Native Contingent and some odd details from the mounted units) he protested that his order from Colonel Glyn on leaving the camp was 'to pull in your defences'. So Durnford left without the two companies, although he obviously intended to take offensive action against the Zulus when he found them. He was an individualist, and probably shared the belief that Lord Chelmsford was, in fact, driving the main Zulu force before him (it has been suggested that small parties of the enemy were deliberately enticing Chelmsford farther away from Isandhlwana) so, by attacking the Zulus in the north-east Durnford hoped to prevent them joining up with their main body; thereby helping Chelmsford.

Durnford left at about 11 a.m. on the 22nd of January. To support him Pulleine sent out A Company to occupy a ridge 1,500 yards north of the camp about an hour later heavy firing was heard from the north-east and soon Captain Shepstone (Colonel Durnford's Staff Officer) galloped in asking urgently for reinforcements for his Basutos who, vastly outnumbered, were being driven back by a huge force of Zulus.

Pulleine reluctantly sent out Captain Mostyn with F Company to reinforce A Company on the northern ridge, then put his camp into a state of readiness. A large force of Zulus now appeared from the east, deployed in their famous crescent formation, while, further north, Durnford's men came into view, fighting a desperate rearguard action as they crossed the front of the camp from Pulleine's left.

A and F Companies on the ridge to the north were now faced with a mass of fast-moving, absolutely silent Zulus into whom they poured steady and accurate fire at 800 yards. But the enemy did not even check, and C Company was pushed out to support the other two, while E, G and H Companies of the 24th and the N.N.C. troops quickly took up defensive positions facing east. Colonel Pulleine's deployment now began to resemble an inverted L, three companies of the 24th facing north, the other two with the HQ details and the guns, east, while the black soldiers of

Dabulamanzi, Cetewayo's brother and leader of the Zulus at Isandhlwana and Ginghilovo.

the N.N.C. fitted into the angle where the two strokes of the L met. They had a vast area to cover but soon brought very heavy and sustained fire upon the advancing Zulus, whose strength has been estimated by various sources as between twenty and thirty thousand (even the most conservative account puts the number in excess of 15,000).

By now the remnants of Durnford's force were at bay in a donga about 800 yards east of the camp, where the left horn of the Impi (the Ngobamakosi 'Boys' Regiment) pitilessly cut them down. The rocket battery had already been slaughtered and it was obvious that there was no hope for the others. The Impi came steadily on, 'a marvellous sight, line upon line of men in extended order one behind the other, bearing all before them.' The experienced soldiers of the 24th (it will be remembered that recently General Cunynghame had praised them for 'their excellence as marksmen') poured volley after volley into the black mass confronting them, exacting a terrible price in Zulu lives, until, at one stage, the attack wavered. But the total discipline of these formidable fighters held; a Zulu cried in a great voice, 'Cetewayo did not tell us to run away!' The attackers rallied, and as the pressure increased the defenders' ammunition began to run out. When the reserve supply was called for a hitch occurred which must have hastened the inevitable end. For the ammunition boxes could not be undone, they were so firmly screwed down that even when the screwdrivers were found only a few could be opened.

Starved of cartridges the firing flagged and suddenly slackened, the Zulus with a savage shout surged forward, and the black soldiers of the N.N.C. broke and fled in terror under the onslaught. The attackers poured into the gap left between the two contingents of the 24th and the climax came with great suddenness; bayonet against assegai, hand to hand, the overwhelming black horde, fifteen or twenty to one, cut the last men down where they stood. Zulu survivors were unanimous in praising the tenacity and valour of the defenders, of whom only three of the 24th left the field alive (Bandsmen Bickley and Wilson and Private Williams, Colonel Glyn's groom, who was ordered by an officer to 'ride for it' on a spare horse).

Just before the end, when defeat was apparent, Colonel Pulleine ordered Lieutenant Melville to save the Queen's Colour of the 1/24th (the Regimental Colour was not present at the battle). Melville fought his way through the thinning end of the Zulu right horn, where he was joined by Lieutenant Coghill, also of the 24th, and together they gained the banks of the swiftly flowing Buffalo River which was in full spate. They tried to cross separately; a Civilian Interpreter called Brickhill has described how Melville, hampered by the Colour, was washed rapidly downstream followed by Coghill who, although he had

The Colour of the 24th rescued from the clutches of the Zulu hordes at the battle of Isandhlwana.

succeeded in reaching the far bank, and despite a badly injured knee, made a gallant attempt to aid him in saving the Colour.

They both reached the Natal bank, but were forced to leave the Colour, which floated downstream into deep water (the pole and crown were later recovered and are now in the Harvard Chapel in Brecon Cathedral). Their bodies, surrounded by dead Zulus, were found next day (both were subsequently awarded posthumous Victoria Crosses). With them perished 21 officers and 534 N.C.O.s and men of the 24th; a harsher blow even than Chillianwala, the carnage of the Great War was not to bring a greater single casualty list—'there were no wounded, no missing, only killed.'

The survivors of the N.N.C. and the other troops who got clear made their way towards the Natal border, which now lay wide open to Cetewayo's conquering Impis.

The post at Rorke's Drift was contained in two store buildings about 40 yards apart, in the compound of the

The graves of Lts. Coghill and Melville at the top of Fugitives Drift. This photograph was taken in 1966 by Major Godwin-Austin, one of whose relatives was killed at Isandhwalana. He was revisiting the scene of the famous battle with a party of soldiers from the 24th who were, until recently, serving in Swaziland . . . the last British troops to do so.

Isandhwalana . . . the battlefield as it is today. Another photograph taken by Major Godwin-Austen. The memorial on the right of the picture is the Regimental Memorial of the 24th.

Swedish Mission. One building housed a hospital containing 36 sick soldiers, the other was a store adjoining a strongly built stone kraal; the whole was surrounded by uncleared brush which could afford good cover to an attacker. The post was manned by B Company of the 2/24th and elements of the N.N.C., under Lieutenant Gonville Bromhead, but the overall command devolved upon Lieutenant Chard, R.E., who had charge of the pontoon bridging the river, and who was senior to Bromhead.

At about 3 p.m. on the 22nd of January, 1879, Lieutenant Adendorff of the N.N.C., who had ridden the 11 miles from Isandhlwana, broke the news of the disaster to Chard. Simultaneously Lieutenant Bromhead received the story from other survivors and at once started to put the post in a state of siege, loopholing and barricading the

The heroic stand of the 24th at Rorke's Drift.

buildings and forming some sort of protective wall out of mealie bags; there was no time to clear the surrounding brush. Shortly afterwards nearly 100 native soldiers of Durnford's Horse arrived from Isandhlwana and placed themselves under Chard's orders, only to ride off in a panic when the first strong force of Zulus appeared. Their terror infected the N.N.C., who left the defences and bolted for Helpmakaar and safety. This left 141 at the post, 30 of whom were sick; almost all the combatant soldiers were from B Company, 2/24th.

The Zulu attack developed quickly, some five hundred of them led by a chief mounted on a grey mare came in at the run as if they expected to surprise the camp. At 500 yards Private Dunbar of B Company picked off the Chief, supported by a fusillade which checked the remainder; but only for a moment. Taking advantage of the broken country and the brush they pressed on to the outer defences, while the few of them who had rifles sniped down at the soldiers from the ridge behind the camp. The garrison remained cool and efficient; despite the enormous odds they shot steadily and accurately as wave after wave of Zulus, 'caring nothing for the slaughter, endeavoured to get over the barricades into the end room of the hospital. Many times Lieutenant Bromhead, collecting a few men, had to drive them off with a bayonet charge. On being repulsed they would retire to better cover, and in a sort of chorus shout and beat their shields with their assegais.' Through all this, Private Joseph Williams, a young soldier with less than two years' service, shot so effectively from the far end of the hospital that next morning 14 dead Zulus were counted immediately below his window, with many more along his line of fire.

Before the front wall the fighting was at its fiercest, the Zulus pressed up to the barricade pulling bayonets from rifles with their bare hands and falling in groups from the controlled volleys of the defenders; their courage was quite extraordinary. Here Mr. Dalton, of the Commissariat, did some effective shooting until he was wounded in the shoulder, then went on encouraging the soldiers and directing their fire. At 6 p.m. the Zulus fired the thatched roof of the hospital and it was during the evacuation of the patients that the true gallantry of the 24th was displayed. Holes had to be cut through the partitions dividing the walls, Private Joseph Williams held the entrance with his bayonet whilst Private John Williams hacked away with an axe until he could pull the patients through into the other room. Joseph Williams was killed before he could clamber through, but one of the cooks (Private Hook) took over and he and John Williams breached three more walls, keeping off the fanatical attackers turn and turn about, until they got the patients out to the comparative safety of the storehouse.

In the next ward, Privates R. Jones and W. Jones, cool and determined as the flames took hold, fought off the Zulus with bullet and bayonet while most of the sick climbed out of the windows. Sergeant Maxfield, one of the 2/24th patients, was delirious with fever and could not move. Private Robert Jones, after seeing the others to safety, returned to the blazing ward to get the Sergeant out; but he was too late, the Zulus were stabbing the N.C.O. to death as he lay in his bed; Robert was lucky to escape with his own life.

The defenders now concentrated around the storehouse, using the illuminating flames to pick off the charging Zulus while two of the walking wounded, Corporal Allen and Private Hitch (the latter's grandson is at present a Captain in the 1st Battalion, The South Wales Borderers), though no longer able to use their rifles, supplied the others with ammunition. Both had been conspicuous in their bravery at the defence of the hospital and they continued to help, despite their wounds, right to the end.

Every man was an example of courage and fortitude,

but among them all Chard and Bromhead, ably supported by the redoubtable Colour-Sergeant Bourne, Sergeants Windridge and Tom Williams (who eventually was mortally wounded), Corporal Schiess (N.N.C.) and Private Roy did sterling service. Chard, with Mr. Dunne of the Commissariat, built a strongpoint of mealie bags in front of the storehouse and from this the defenders brought a withering all-round fire to bear on the black fanatics rushing into the flame-lit scene from the enveloping darkness. At last, around midnight, the attack tailed off; cautiously, Chard and Bromhead allowed some of the defenders to rest at their posts.

When dawn came the enemy had withdrawn; by the time Lord Chelmsford's column appeared in sight at 8 a.m. the area was being vigorously patrolled and the defences overhauled. At a cost of only 17 killed or died of wounds, and 10 wounded, 450 Zulu dead were found; while many were carried off on the shields of their retreating comrades. What made them go? Had they stomached enough, with their appalling losses, or were they aware of Chelmsford's approach? Whatever the reason, the immediate threat to Natal's borders had been lifted, and for this the 24th are remembered in South Africa to this day.

It must have been extremely difficult to select from the roll of this small, gallant band (who had faced and outfought the 3,000-strong Zulu Undi Corps) the names to be put forward for honours and awards. Lieutenants Chard and Bromhead both received the Victoria Cross and Brevet-Majorities, while the V.C. went also to Corporal Allen, Privates Hitch, Hook, R. Jones, W. Jones and John Williams, all of the 24th. The V.C. was awarded to Surgeon-Major Reynolds for his arduous and exacting hospital work under appalling conditions, and to Assistant-Commissary Dalton and Corporal Schiess of the Natal Native Contingent. Private Roy received the D.C.M., as

2nd Battalion "24th Regiment."

ROLL OF "B" COMPANY who defended "RORKE'S DRIFT" against the Zulu attack on the night of the 22nd-23rd January, 1879.

Regtl. No.	Rank.	Name.	Remarks.
	Lieutenant	BROMHEAD, GONVILLE (V.C.)	Mentioned in Dispatches. Awarded the Victoria Cross.
2459	Color-Sergt.	BOURNE, F.	Mentioned in Dispatches. Awarded the Distinguished Conduct Medal.
735	Sergeant	WINDRIDGE, J. L.	Mentioned in Dispatches.
81	Sergeant	GALLAGHER, H. L.	
1387	Sergeant	SMITH, G.	
849	Sergeant	SAXTY. A.	
1328	Lce.Sergt.	WILLIAMS, T.	Mentioned in Dispatches. Died of Wounds 23rd Jan., 1879.
82	Corporal	TAYLOR, J.	
1240	Corporal	ALLAN, W. W. (V.C.)	Wounded Severely. Awarded the Victoria Cross.
582	Corporal	FRENCH, J.	
2350	Corporal	BUSH, J.	
1282	Lce.Corpl.	HALLEY, J.	
1287	Lce.Corpl.	BISSELL, W.	
2389	Lce.Corpl.	KEY, J.	
1618	Lce.Corpl.	SHERMAN, G.	
2067	Drummer	HAYES, P.	
2381	Drummer	KEEFE, J.	
912	Private	ASHTON, J.	
1381	Private	BARRY, T.	
918	Private	BENNETT, W.	
2427	Private	BLY, J.	
1402	Private	BUCK, W.	
1184	Private	BUCKLEY, T.	
1220	Private	BURKE, T.	
2420	Private	CAINE, P.	
1181	Private	CAMP, W. H.	
1241	Private	CHESTER, T.	
755	Private	CLAYTON, F.	
801	Private	COLE, T.	Killed 22nd January, 1879.
1396	Private	COLLINS, T.	
1323	Private	CONNORS, T.	
2310	Private	CONNORS, H.	
470	Private	DAVIES, G.	
1363	Private	DAVIES, W. H.	
1178	Private	DAW, T.	
1467	Private	DEACON, G.	
1357	Private	DEANE, W.	
1697	Private	DICKS, W.	
971	Private	DRISCOLL, T.	
1421	Private	DUNBAR, J.	
922	Private	EDWARDS, G.	
969	Private	FAGAN, J.	Killed 22nd January, 1879.

Regtl. No.	Rank.	Name.	Remarks.
2429	Private	GEE, E.	
1362	Private	HITCH, F. (V.C.)	Wounded Severely. Awarded the Victoria Cross.
1373	Private	HOOK, H. (V.C.)	Mentioned in Dispatches. Awarded the Victoria Cross.
1061	Private	JOBBINS, J.	
1428	Private	JONES, E.	
970	Private	JONES, J.	
1179	Private	JONES, J.	
716	Private	JONES, R. (V.C.)	Mentioned in Dispatches. Awarded the Victoria Cross.
593	Private	JONES, W. (V.C.)	Mentioned in Dispatches. Awarded the Victoria Cross.
2437	Private	JUDGE, P.	
972	Private	KEARS, P.	
1386	Private	KILEY, M.	
963	Private	LEWIS, D.	
1409	Private	LLOYD, D.	
1304	Private	LODGE, J.	
942	Private	LYNCH, T.	
756	Private	MARTIN, H.	
1284	Private	MASON, C.	
1527	Private	MINEHAN, M.	
968	Private	MOFFATT, T.	
525	Private	MORRIS, F.	
1342	Private	MORRIS, A.	
1371	Private	MORRISON, T.	
1257	Private	NORRIS, R.	
1480	Private	OSBORNE, W.	
1399	Private	PARRY, S.	
1286	Private	ROBINSON, T.	
1065	Private	RUCK, J.	
914	Private	SHERGOLD, J.	
1005	Private	SMITH, J.	
1812	Private	TASKER, W.	
973	Private	TAYLOR, F.	
889	Private	TAYLOR, T.	
879	Private	TOBIN, M.	
1281	Private	TODD, W. G.	
1315	Private	TONGUE, R.	
1497	Private	WALL, J.	
977	Private	WHITTON, A.	
1187	Private	WILCOX, W.	
1395	Private	WILLIAMS, J. (V.C.)	Mentioned in Dispatches. Awarded the Victoria Cross.
1374	Private	WILLIAMS, J.	
1398	Private	WILLIAMS, J.	Killed 22nd January, 1879.
1060	Private	WILLIAMS, T.	

The following Officers and N. C. Officers were attached to above Company.

1st Battalion, 24th Regiment.
Private W. BECKETT .. .. Killed—H.
Private W. HARRIGAN .. .. Killed—H.
Private M. JENKINS .. .. Killed—H.
Private W. NICHOLAS .. .. Killed—H.
Private J. WILLIAMS .. .. Killed—H.
Private ROY .. Mentioned in Dispatches.

2nd Battalion, 24th Regiment.
Sergeant R. MAXFIELD .. Killed—H.
Private R. ADAMS .. .. Killed—H.
Private J. CHICK .. .. Killed—H.
Private G. HAYDEN .. .. Killed—H.
Private J. SCANLON .. .. Killed—H.

Royal Artillery.
Bombardier LEWIS.. .. .. H.

Royal Engineers.
Lieutenant JOHN R. M. CHARD (V.C.).
Mentioned in Dispatches.
Awarded the Victoria Cross.

The Buffs.
Sergeant MILNE.

Commissariat Department.
Asst. Commissary DUNNE,
Mentioned in Dispatches.
Acting Commst. Officer DALTON,
Severely Wounded.
Mentioned in Dispatches.
Acting Store-keeper BYRNE .. Killed.
Mentioned in Dispatches.
Corporal ATTWOOD.
Awarded the Distinguished Conduct Medal.

Army Hospital Corps.
Surgeon REYNOLDS (V.C.),
Mentioned in Dispatches.
Awarded the Victoria Cross.
Private McMAHON,
Mentioned in Dispatches.

Natal Mounted Police.
Trooper HUNTER .. .. .. Killed—H.
Trooper GREEN .. .. .. Killed—H.

Natal Native Contingent.
Corporal SCHIESS (V.C.).. Severely Wounded.
Mentioned in Dispatches.
Awarded the Victoria Cross.
Corporal MAYER .. .. H.
Corporal SCAMMELL.

Chaplain's Department.
Revd. C. SMITH .. .. Acting Chaplain.

Civilian .. Mr. DANIELS.

Note.—Those N. C. Officers and Men marked with an "H" indicate they were patients in Hospital.

Rorke's Drift. The roll of honour compiled from the pay records by Major F. Bourne who as a Colour Sergeant in B Company played such a distinguished part in the fight.

A contemporary song sheet. Notice the black armband.

did Colour-Sergeant Bourne, who afterwards gained a Commission.*

The 2/24th rebuilt the post at Rorke's Drift; they called it 'Fort Revenge' but later Lord Chelmsford had it changed to the 'more appropriate' name of Fort Melville. Even so, for the men of the 24th it was Revenge, for they considered that Rorke's Drift had atoned for the disaster of Isandhlwana. And for others, too, it was a moral victory, it proved that the Zulus could be beaten, that their menace could be overcome; as indeed it finally was at

* The Author had the honour of speaking to Colonel Bourne, then a still active man, at the Northern Command Tattoo in July 1934.

Queen Victoria decorates the recovered colour of 24th the at Osborne House.

Ulundi in July 1879. For the Regiment, this remains its greatest honour:

'The Defence of Rorke's Drift is Immortal.'

CHAPTER TEN

1879-1914

THE SOUTH AFRICAN WAR of 1900–1902 was not to have the same impact on the Regiment as the tremendous incidents of 1879, though the years between held many memorable events. In April, 1879, in action against the Zulus in the Inhobana mountains, Lieutenant E. S. Browne, operating under Colonel Wood with a detachment of 1/24th Mounted Infantry, gained the Regiment's sixteenth Victoria Cross rescuing a soldier under the very noses of the enemy. The 1st Battalion's lost Colour had been found in the Buffalo River by the party commanded by Major Black of the 24th which had previously found the bodies of Lieutenants Melvill and Coghill.

Her Majesty was soon to see this historic Colour in person. On 28th July, 1880, at Osborne in the Isle of Wight, she attached a wreath of immortelles to its pike and later, through the Adjutant-General, directed that 'as a lasting token of her act in placing a wreath on the Queen's Colour to commemorate the devotion displayed by Lieutenants Melvill and Coghill in their heroic endeavour to save the Colour on January 22nd, 1879, and of the noble defence of Rorke's Drift, Her Majesty has been graciously pleased to command that a silver wreath shall in future be borne around the staff of the Queen's Colours of both battalions of the 24th Regiment'. The pole, case and crown of one of the 2/24th's lost Colours was also recovered and was presented to Queen Victoria in person by Major C. J. Bromhead for safe-keeping in the Armoury at Windsor Castle.

The 1/24th had embarked for Portsmouth from South Africa in August 1879 to spend 13 years in the United Kingdom, six of them in Ireland, before leaving for Egypt at the end of 1892. During this time the Colours of the Regiment were enriched by the battle-honour 'South Africa' in February 1881 and the following year (at long last) the Marlborough victories of 'Blenheim', 'Ramillies', 'Oudenarde' and 'Malplaquet'; a year later the dates 1877–8–9 were added to 'South Africa'.

When, on the 1st of July 1881, the Regiment changed its title from Second Warwickshire to the 'South Wales Borderers' the transformation was made quickly and easily. Both battalions bore the same number and the Regiment, which was universally known as the 24th (as it is today), had been based on Brecon for the past eight years, recruiting in South Wales and along the Welsh Border. One reflection of the change was the official adoption of the 'Men of Harlech' as the Regimental March, while 'Warwickshire Lads' was retained for use on ceremonial occasions.

There were two changes in the Colonelcy: Sir Charles Ellice succeeded Pringle Taylor in April 1884 and was, on his death in November 1888, replaced by General Wodehouse (both officers having had distinguished service in the 24th).

The 2/24th stayed on for a while in South Africa after the 1st Battalion had gone, then left for Gibraltar where, in the Queen's name, new Colours were presented by Lord Napier of Magdala. 'The Colours of your Regiment have been unfurled in every quarter of the globe,' said Lord Napier, 'in America, Egypt, South Africa, Spain, Portugal and India; and the history of your Regiment is one of which you may well be proud. It is a noble heritage.' After an uneventful stay on 'the Rock' the 2/24th travelled to India, arriving at Bombay on the 1st of September, 1882, moving first to Poona, then to Secunderabad and later to Madras, where they once more provided the Andaman Islands detachment.

In 1886 they started on a spell of active service in Burma, where King Theebaw had been at loggerheads with the British Government for some time. Theebaw was deposed after a swift campaign, but when the 2/24th arrived in Rangoon in May they found widespread insurrection and was soon split into detachments spread over a wide area with Headquarters at Thayet-Myo. The elusive Burmese dacoits proved a troublesome enemy. The British deployed a force of 24,000 against them in what became known as the 'Subalterns War', a hit-and-run affair of ambush and counter-ambush similar to the Malayan campaign in which the Regiment was to fight 70 years later. The 2/24th's two and a half years in Burma cost them more casualties from sickness than from the enemy. They must have been glad to get back to India, where they stayed from November 1888 until October 1892.

Then, for the first time, the 24th did a one-year tour in Aden, an unpleasant spot which they were to see again in the years to come (in 1928 and 1967). Lieutenant-Colonel Browne, V.C. was now in command, having taken over from Colonel Penn Symons (both names are well known from Zulu War days). Browne brought the 2/24th back to England where they stayed, mainly in the south, until, on July the 9th, 1897 they travelled to South Wales, arriving at Newport to start a recruiting march of some 136 days that took them through place-names which have a familiar ring: first stage, Pontypool to Glanusk to Brecon; then Llandovery, Carmarthen and Tenby (poaching from the Welch Regiment?) and so on to their new station of Pembroke Dock.

When the South African War started the 1/24th were in

India, having moved there in 1897 afer a spell in Gibraltar. General Wodehouse had died in May 1898, and much to everybody's satisfaction, Lieutenant-General Glyn became Colonel of the Regiment. At about the same time the Regiment took a new cap badge into use; it was the Sphinx, superscribed 'Egypt', surrounded by a gilt wreath of immortelles in memory of the Isandhlwana battle and the Defence of Rorke's Drift; on this wreath the letters 'S.W.B.' were imposed. The officers' badge was identical, except that it was smaller and made of silver.

The 2nd Battalion arrived in South Africa from Ireland in time to join in Lord Roberts' operations for the relief of Kimberley in February and March 1900 (having already sent a Mounted Infantry detachment 34 strong with the expeditionary force six months earlier). The enemy successes caused two more divisions to be sent out from England; the 2/24th went into 15 Brigade, part of the Seventh Division, with the 2nd Cheshires, 1st East Lancashire and 2nd North Staffordshire.

Their first action was at Jacobsdal on the 15th of February on the way to the Modder River as part of Lord Roberts' force to relieve Kimberley. Shortly afterwards General Cronje surrendered with over 4,000 Boers but, although the M.I. Companies were present, the remainder of the 2nd Battalion were not committed. Lord Roberts then pressed on towards Bloemfontein, marching in three columns with the 2/24th, still in the Seventh Division, in the right-hand column. The going was soft and boggy but even so on one day (March 6th) they covered 23 miles, arriving at Bloemfontein to find it undefended. Roberts then attacked the Boers at Karee siding, where the battalion came under fire as they advanced up the railway line in extended order to attack the enemy. The wire fence protecting the railway caused some delay but the 2/24th behaved 'very steadily, advancing and lying down under fire like an Aldershot field-day'.

The enemy did not wait for the Seventh Division's full attack to develop and the best the soldiers could do was to try to wing the rapidly retreating Boers as they rode down the reverse slope of the hill to fall back on to Brandfort. Casualties were surprisingly light, less than 200 for the whole Division (the battalion lost three men killed and 1 officer and 23 wounded).

The campaign was rapidly developing into guerilla warfare with its ephemeral, though still lethal, encounters; flying columns and M.I. raids, barbed wire and blockhouses and isolated, often heroic, actions of which the battalion had its share. When peace was signed at Vereeniging on the 31st of May 1902 the 2/24th had sustained 216 casualties, 95 of them from disease. They had earned the battle-honour 'South Africa 1900–1902' and individual honours which included a C.B. (for Colonel Roche), 4 D.S.O.s, 11 D.C.M.s and 24 mentions in dispatches.

This account would not be complete without a mention of the Volunteer Battalions of the South Wales Borderers, who supplied one company of volunteers to the 2/24th throughout the campaign; these were the 1st (Brecknockshire) Battalion and the 2nd, 3rd, 4th and 5th Volunteer Battalions. In addition to these the 3rd (Militia) Battalion was called up and sent to Dublin to relieve the 2nd Battalion; while there they volunteered almost to a man and fought in South Africa from March 1900 for two years. This was the battalion who had held the title 'The Royal South Wales Borderers Militia Rifles' until the Reforms of 1881, when they bequeathed part of their name to the Regiment.

The 2/24th stayed in South Africa on garrison duty until May 1904, and returned there after spending six years in England mainly on the periphery of Salisbury Plain and in Aldershot. During this time the Regiment received authority to resume the grass-green facings (dating back to their days as 'Howard's Greens') from which they had been reluctantly parted in 1881. While at Cape Town many visits were paid to Isandhlwana and Rorke's Drift, but the battalion missed the unveiling of the Memorial because of their posting in 1912 to North China, where at Tientsin they joined the International Force, serving alongside Germans who were soon to be their enemies in the conflagration of 1914.

General Glyn, one of the Regiment's most notable Colonels, died in November, 1900 and was succeeded by General Degacher, who had commanded the 2nd Battalion in Zululand. The 1/24th had then seen out a quarter of their thirteen-year tour in India, spending some of the time on the North West Frontier, where the repercussions of the Boer War were hardly felt. Shortly before leaving for home they sent a large draft off to South Africa (where they were to wait for the 2nd Battalion's arrival from England on their 1910 tour).

The 1st Battalion settled into Chatham, feeling their way slowly among the changes and innovations that had taken place during their absence. The 'new-fangled' aeroplane had not yet found a military use but the motor-car was past the novelty stage and was being tried out as a means of transportation, although few thought it would ever replace the horse. A new Territorial Force had been formed and Regular Units at home were re-organized and re-equipped on an 'Expeditionary Force' basis. It was under these conditions while training at Bordon as a part of 3 Brigade in the First Division, that the outbreak of the Great War found them.

CHAPTER ELEVEN

1914–1918

THE BUILD-UP of naval and military power after the Franco-German War had paved the way for a head-on clash between the forces of Kaiser Wilhelm II and most of the European powers, particularly France and Russia. The Germans hoped that they could deal separately with these two great nations while Britain remained a neutral onlooker, but this was not to be. When, in June, 1914, the Archduke Ferdinand and his wife were assassinated at Sarajevo, it was inevitable that England would be involved.

The Great War was fought on a vast scale, it was the first global war. The exploits of the two Regular battalions of the 24th Regiment in the period 1914–1918 require a book to themselves, without taking into account the Territorial and Service Units, who between them raised 16 battalions. The full history of the Regiment in the Great War is made up of the efforts of all the members of the Corps of The South Wales Borderers, whether active or draft-finding, garrison soldiers or front-line troops; their several records of service are recorded by Professor Atkinson in his History published by the Medici Society in 1931. All that can be attempted here is a short résumé of the major engagements in which the 1st and 2nd Battalions took part, with brief accounts of other, outstanding, contributions.

Within three weeks of the outbreak of hostilities on the 4th of August, 1914, the 1st Battalion was in action at Mons. They were part of the Army that the Kaiser dismissed, ironically, as 'contemptible'; and they suffered the toil and hardship of the great Retreat without the satisfaction of seeing real action against the enemy.

But on the Aisne on the 14th of September they got the opportunity to strike back. After checking (with the Welch) a German counter-attack on the Beaulne ridge the battalion advanced up the Chivy valley to carry out a most gallant attack which cost them 150 casualities, afterwards holding the open ground on the slopes of the Chemin des Dames against continual counter-attack. Twelve days later, on the tactically important Mont Faucon spur, during desperate combat in which men actually fought with fists and one even used a table fork to defend himself, the battalion held their ground against the most determined and formidable of the German counter-attacks made during the entire Aisne battle. They were thanked by Sir Douglas Haig who was their Corps Commander during the battle, 'The conduct of the South Wales Borderers in driving back the strong attack made upon them,' he wrote, 'is particularly deserving of praise.'

At the end of October 1914 the battalion, having been forced back with the rest of the 1st Division by the impetus of the German drive towards the Channel Ports, found themselves holding an area in front of Gheluvelt Château.

The weather was foul, driving rain and thick mud hampered communications with the Welch Regiment around nearby Gheluvelt village and with the Scots Guards on the battalion's left flank. During the night of the 31st October sporadic sniping preceded a severe artillery bombardment, which was closely followed by repeated infantry attacks, particularly against C Company, who were on the right of the line, nearest the Welch. The battalion held their ground and even succeeded in taking some prisoners, while all around them the enemy infantry flooded through the British defences, overwhelming the Welch and many other Units. Lieutenant-Colonel Burleigh Leach, the

Battalion Commander, had already distinguished himself many times during the night, and now, with C Company overrun and their commander killed, he counter-attacked through the Château grounds with the remnants of two of his companies, some men of battalion headquarters and details of the Scots Guards.

The surprised Germans broke and ran, enabling A and D Companies, with the Scots Guards, to inflict considerable execution while Colonel Leach moved up to the edge of the Château grounds, where the right flank was wide open. Gheluvelt village was now in enemy hands and the battalion's right rear was being heavily bombarded. It was at this stage that the famous counter-attack of the 2nd Worcestershire's under Major Hankey threw the Germans out of Gheluvelt Château, for the moment stabilizing the British line. Both battalions suffered heavy casualties, and to this day honour their shared achievement with pride by exchanging greetings on Gheluvelt's anniversary. The 1st Battalion fought in France throughout the whole of the war, remaining in the 1st Division through the bitter trench warfare of 1915, the hardships of the Somme in the following year and of Ypres in 1917. Nowhere did they fight harder or with more gallantry than at Gheluvelt, which ranks with Talavera and Rorke's Drift among the great achievements of the Regiment.

In 1918, after the breaking of the Hindenburg Line, an armistice was declared on November the 11th. Soon afterwards the 1st Battalion marched across the Rhine into Germany, carrying with them the Colour that was saved at Isandhlwana.

We left the 2nd Battalion in China where they formed part of the International garrison at Tientsin. In September 1914, supported by a half-battalion of the 36th Sikhs, they sailed to join their Allies, the Japanese, in an expedition against the German-occupied territory of Kiaochau,

Reproduced by permission of the Worcestershire Regiment

Gheluvelt, October 14th, 1914. The Worcestershires come to the aid of the 24th in the nick of time.

with its port of Tsingtao. They encountered little hard fighting (the total casualities amounted to about fifty all ranks) but the extremely arduous conditions and the bad weather caused them great discomfort. When Tsingtao fell on the 7th of November it brought the unusual distinction of a battle-honour held by no other British regiment.

The battalion came home to Devonport in January 1915, moving soon to Rugby where they became part of 87 Brigade in the 29th Division (the junior of the so-called 'Old Army' Divisions); they stayed in this formation for the remainder of the Great War. The battalion trained hard, expecting at any time to be sent to France, but the need for a diversion in the Mediterranean found the whole Division in April, 1915, heading east towards Gallipoli with the object of securing an open passage for Allied ships through the Helles Straits to the Black Sea.

The historical 'Landing at Helles' ranks high in the annals of the Regiment. On the 25th of April the 2nd Battalion took part in an assault on open beaches, landing three companies in broad daylight in the face of a determined and well-prepared enemy. The cost was comparatively light when reckoned against some of the other units of the 29th Division (a total of 62 casualities), but A Company, who landed unsuccessfully on 'Y' beach with the K.O.S.B. and the Marines, sustained more casualities, including its Company Commander, than the other three put together before it was forced to withdraw. The three companies moved from 'S' beach, on Morto Bay, up towards Krithia as part of an attack which never got into its stride because of the main advance becoming held up at Sedd el Bahr. The whole force fought desperately to maintain its foothold against the ferocious counter-attacks of the Turks (who were allies of the Germans), and despite heavy losses remained on Cape Helles during May and June. In August they moved with the rest of 29th Division

Gallipoli, 1915. A message from Ian Hamilton.

to Suvla Bay, where a new landing by five divisions fresh from England had been brought to a halt. Here, at Scimitar Hill, they took part in a desperate attack which failed against the fierce resistance of the Turks and cost the 2nd Battalion nearly 300 casualities. By October they were back at Helles, where the fighting degenerated into trench warfare for the remaining few months of the campaign. In January, 1916, there was a general evacuation from the Gallipoli Peninsula, the 'Immortal Gamble' had failed; the 2nd Battalion, with the 29th Division, was sent to Egypt, having lost almost 1,600 officers and men in less than nine months.

Their stay in Egypt was short. In March, 1916, the 29th Division moved to France and the 2nd Battalion saw their first major action on the Somme in July during the attack on the 'impregnable' position of Beaufort Hamel. Advancing in the leading line they were literally mown down by the massed machine-gun fire of the enemy but some gallant soldiers struggled on to within reach of the German wire before the attack failed all along the line. The Division suffered heavily, the 2nd Battalion's casualties alone amounting in the first few minutes to 11 officers and 235 men killed and missing and 4 officers and 149 wounded out of a total of 21 officers and 578 men.

This became the tragic pattern of the Great War, units were cut to pieces and reformed only to be decimated in the next attack. The battalion was reconstituted and fought in various parts of the Line, nowhere more gallantly than at Monchy Le Preux in April and May 1917. It was at Monchy on May the 19th, that Sergeant F. White gained a posthumous Victoria Cross in attempting to silence enemy machine-guns holding up the advance of D Company. Seeing that both Company officers were killed Sergeant White, supported by Corporal Nowel, attacked the nearest machine-gun nest, shooting three Germans and bayoneting a fourth before going down mortally wounded under a hail of fire.

Through the desperate 'Third Ypres' during the summer and autumn of 1917 the battalion fought on, until in November and December they played a memorable, perhaps their most gallant, part in the War at the battle of Cambrai. The Germans thought their carefully prepared Hindenburg Line, backed by its massive support, to be impregnable. Behind these a third defensive line ran through Beaurevoir-Masnières, while the Scheldt Canal provided another obstacle to the taking of Cambrai.

But the Allies knew that the area was favourable for the movement of tanks, whose use in mass for the first time was sure to gain them the initiative, aided by their unique ability to cut through the mass of enemy barbed wire which provided the main obstacle to the infantry. At first light on the 20th of November 1917, four hundred tanks, followed by three divisions and covered by a massive artillery barrage smashed through the Hindenburg Line and the Support Line. The 29th Division followed to secure the crossing of the Scheldt Canal and make the way clear for the storming of the Beaurevoir Line some 1,500 yards further on.

A and C Companies of the 2nd Battalion were at first pinned down on one of the canal locks but managed to force a crossing, thus allowing the Inniskillings, assisted by C Company, to attack the Beaurevoir Line, but they just failed to reach it. Early next morning the battalion renewed the attack, going forward with the K.O.S.B. until the latter were held up, as were 86 Brigade, leaving the South Wales Borderers unable to hold their objective against repeated enemy counter-attacks which eventually drove them back to Battalion Headquarters, where they rallied and fought the Germans off.

A spell out of the Line followed, then, barely 48 hours after the battalion had taken up their new positions covering Marcoing, the Germans attacked in great strength in a determined attempt to capture the canal bridgeheads. They fought under heavy artillery and small-arms fire with little rest or food until they were relieved by the Hampshires on the evening of the 3rd of December. Then they marched wearily out of the Line behind Lieutenant-Colonel G. T. Raikes their gallant C.O.: two officers, the doctor and 73 men, all that was left of a battalion.

The 2nd Battalion stayed in France until the end of the Great War, taking part in many actions. They fought on the Lys and helped to recapture Gheluvelt, where their comrades of the 1st Battalion had made their great stand. Their steadfastness and courage at the great battle of Cambrai was to be recorded for posterity, for its name is now emblazoned on the Colours that were carried into Germany with the victorious British Army of Occupation.

The 4th Battalion fought with the 2nd at Gallipoli, where they lost the officer who had trained them and led them into battle, Lieutenant-Colonel F. M. Gillespie. After the evacuation they served in Mesopotamia, where in 1916 Captain Buchanan and Private Fynn both won the Victoria Cross, the first for saving a wounded officer and then a soldier under heavy fire, and the other, a few days later, for rescuing two men in broad daylight within 300 yards of the Turkish Lines.

The 5th and 6th Battalion served, mainly as Pioneers, in France during the war while 7th and 8th after a spell of duty in France both served in Macedonia. The 10th and 11th (the 'Gwent') Battalions went to France with the 38th Division and stayed until the end of the war. C.S.M. Jack Williams, of Ebbw Vale, won the 10th Battalion's V.C. at Villers Outreaux, in a most gallant action assisted by Private R. Evans, who received the D.C.M. Jack Williams, one of the Regiment's great heroes, finished the war with the V.C., D.C.M., M.M. and Bar and the Médaille Militaire, which must be unique. The 11th Battalion got their Victoria Cross through Sergeant Ivor Rees, who rushed a machine-gun nest, silenced the gun and accounted for two of its handlers before going on to bomb an adjacent pillbox, where he killed five of the occupants and took the other 32 prisoner.

The 12th Battalion, formed as 'Bantams', went to France in June 1916 and was disbanded two years later. The 9th, 13th and 14th Battalions were draft-finding units and saw no active service, while the 51st, 52nd and 53rd were 'Young Soldier' Battalions formed in 1918 for ser-

Men of the 24th on their way up to the front line, near Montauban, October, 1916.

vice in the Army of Occupation. The Territorial Battalions of Brecknock and Monmouth contributed gallantly to the war effort of the Corps of the South Wales Borderers, serving in many countries and on the main fronts. It would take many thousands of words to tell of their triumphs and disasters and to recount their severe casualties.

The Regiment's final Victoria Cross of the Great War was won by Lieutenant-Colonel D. G. Johnson, who at the time was commanding the 2nd Battalion of the Royal Sussex Regiment, fighting almost alongside the 1st South Wales Borderers near Fesmy, in France, not long before the Armistice came. This brought the number of Victoria Crosses won in that war to six, and the Regiment's total to twenty-two. Many other decorations and awards were won and 74 battle-honours were awarded, ten of them to be borne on the Colours ('Mons'; 'Marne 1914'; 'Ypres,

C.S.M. Jack Williams V.C., D.C.M., M.M. and Bar, one of the most decorated soldiers of World War I. Although it is not shown he was also awarded the Médaille Militaire.

1914, 17, 18'; 'Gheluvelt'; 'Somme, 1916, 18'; 'Cambrai, 1917, 18'; 'Doiran, 1917, 18'; 'Landing at Helles'; 'Baghdad' and 'Tsingtao').

Mere words are inadequate to express the gallantry and devotion to duty of the officers and men of the Regiment who suffered the carnage, filth and discomfort of the 'Great War to end Wars'. The spirit of the 24th shines through their exploits, and the dry, 'dead-pan' outlook of 1914–18 could not be better expressed than through the closing words of the 1st Battalion's Diary on receiving the news of the Armistice, out of the Line, on November the 11th, 1918: 'Training was washed out and the battalion washed its feet.'

CHAPTER TWELVE

1919–1945

THE PERIOD BETWEEN the two wars was not particularly peaceful for the 24th. The 1st Battalion was involved in the Irish 'troubles' of 1920–1922, where the wild Rapparees of 1690 were now replaced by their lineal descendants, the Sinn Feiners. A six-year spell in England followed during which, on August the 11th, 1922, H.R.H. the Prince of Wales was appointed the first Colonel-in-Chief of the Regiment; a widely popular choice. Another highlight was the winning of the Army Rugby Cup for four successive years (in the seasons between 1924 and 1928) a feat which has only once been equalled.

The battalion moved to Cairo in 1928 but in less than a year two companies were flown down to Palestine where the Jewish 'Zionist' policies were being militantly opposed by the Arabs. The rest of the battalion followed, leaving a company behind in Cairo, and for some four months kept the peace over a wide area of the Holy Land before returning to Egypt at the end of 1929. In October the following year they sailed to Hong Kong for a four-year tour during which new Colours were presented to replace the famous Isandhlwana set (these being sent back to Brecon to be laid up in the Havard Chapel at the Cathedral). The new Colours were the first to carry the new centre badge granted by King George V: 'Within a wreath of immortelles the Roman numeral XXIV'.

The battalion regretfully left Hong Kong for India in November 1934, joining 1st (Abbotabad) Brigade of the

The Prince of Wales, a photograph taken in 1922.

1st Indian Division, the rest of the brigade consisting of Gurkha Regiments, in Rawalpindi. They missed the Mohmand campaign the following summer, but were quickly committed when, in February 1937, the Wazirs,

Ceremonial duty between the wars. Drum-major Matthews of the Second Battalion and an unidentified drummer boy.

under the turbulent Faqir of Ipi, ambushed a British Column, causing severe casualties. They then moved up to Mir Ali, a camp just inside Tribal territory, with the remainder of the Abbotabad Brigade. Lieutenant-Colonel G. A. Brett, D.S.O., O.B.E., M.C., has vividly described in his 1937–1952 History how the battalion fared against tough frontier tribesmen in mountainous terrain which sometimes resembled a lunar landscape.

When the campaign ended, eleven months later, the comparatively light casualties (4 killed and 23 wounded) belied the gallantry displayed by all ranks in this small but arduous mountain war. The honour that pleased the battalion most was the unofficial one conferred upon it by its comrades of the Abbotabad Brigade: the nickname of 'the White Gurkhas'.

The 1st Battalion stayed on the Frontier until October 1939, when it moved to Cawnpore from Landi Kotal amid 'alarums of war' spreading eastwards from Europe.

The 2nd Battalion had moved to India in 1919 and there they stayed on routine duties, until 1927. During this eight-year tour General George Paton died and his place as Colonel of the Regiment was taken by Sir Alexander Cobbe, V.C., G.C.B., K.C.S.I., D.S.O. The battalion left Bombay for Aden at the end of 1927 and established their headquarters in the Crater (now, tragically, a household name); but even then, because of the heat, the area was known as 'Hell with the lid off'. They sent off a large draft to strengthen the 1st Battalion, in Cairo, in September 1928 and four months later sailed for home in the H.T. *Nevasa*, leaving Aden to be garrisoned by the Royal Air Force. The 2nd Battalion went into the 9th Infantry Brigade in the Portsmouth area, soon to be commanded by Brigadier Ll. I. G. Morgan-Owen, who became Colonel of the Regiment when General Sir Alexander Cobbe, V.C., died in June 1931. The next three years were spent in Catterick Camp, in Yorkshire, where the autumn training cycle in 1935 was interrupted by the sudden departure of the battalion to Malta, when the tension built up by Mussolini's bid for power in Abyssinia caused the garrison there to be strengthened. Before long a more urgent call came, and in mid-July 1936 they moved to Palestine where the Arab General Strike had escalated into active guerilla operations against the Jews. The 2nd Battalion went into the Southern Brigade, operating mainly around Sarafand, Jaffa and Tel Aviv, and providing detachments for railway and convoy duties. In October the tide turned against the Arabs and at the end of 1936 the battalion sailed for Londonderry in Northern Ireland. There, under the command of Lieutenant-Colonel D. H. S. Somerville, M.C., they celebrated the 250th Anniversary of the founding of the Regiment (28th March 1939) by trooping the Colour in the presence of the Governor, the Duke of Abercorn; while, in Europe, Hitler's hordes were on the march.

The onset of the 1939 War left the British Army in India, including the 1st Battalion, in a backwater disturbed only by sporadic outbreaks of communal rioting. The battalion was not fully mobilized until August, 1941, but when they left India for Iraq in November they were up to strength and ready for any eventuality (having been described by the General Officer Commanding-in-Chief as 'one of the two best battalions in India').

The threat to the oilfields of Iraq by the German forces operating against the Russians in the Caucasus caused the battalion to move to Qaiyara, in Northern Iraq, and then to Mosul, mostly engaged in digging defences in deplorable weather. By now they were part of 20 Indian Brigade of 10th Indian Division, moving with it on 24th May, 1942 to Egypt via Transjordan and Palestine, eventually arriving at Bir Hamid, just east of Tobruk, on 5th June after one of the longest approach marches into battle in the history of warfare, some 1,500 miles in twelve days.

The German offensive under Rommel was in full swing, and as the battalion reconnoitred their defensive positions with the 3/18th Garwhal Rifles and the 1/6th Rajputana Rifles they could clearly hear the bitter battles being fought in the nearby 'Cauldron'. Digging-in was difficult, hard rock lay barely two feet below the sand, but extensive minefields were laid around the perimeter while the M.T. was concentrated in the shelter of a ridge to the rear of the position. By the time Lieutenant-Colonel F. R. G.

Matthews arrived on 11th June, to take over command, the battalion was patrolling the area extensively in trucks and carriers.

Several forays were made outside the defensive 'Box' but little contact was made with the Germans, although there was some shelling and mortar exchanges on 14th/15th June. On the 16th the enemy attacked the Rajputana Rifles at Sidi Rezegh, overrunning the Indian battalion and forcing the remnants to withdraw from the ridge. Early the next day the 1st Battalion sent out patrols to Sidi Rezegh to find that the Germans had continued their advance to the south-east; the patrols brought back two prisoners and salvaged what they could of the Indian regiment's motor transport.

Tobruk was still holding out, indeed the overall plan was to defend the 'Box' to the bitter end, but on the evening of 17th June the two remaining battalions of the Brigade were ordered to withdraw to Sollum, some 70 miles to the east. The 1st Battalion Intelligence Officer was captured while reconnoitring the ten-mile route to the waiting transport, and this added to the difficulties caused by the sudden decision to withdraw by 10 p.m. that night. The few usable vehicles were loaded up and the marching troops cautiously edged their way through a gap in the minefield covered by a small rearguard under Major C. P. G. de Winton.

The battalion paused in the gathering darkness at the foot of the escarpment and a compass route was plotted on the 'left hand bottom star of the constellation of Cassiopeia', which brought the battalion safely to the rendezvous with the transport on the Gambut road. Silently the tired men embussed and at 0300 hours on 18th June moved off 'on the journey which was to end in the battalion's virtual extinction'. For within the hour, nearing Gambut, the convoy ran into a confused mêlée of vehicles straddling the road.

At first it was thought that a German patrol had cut the track and the battalion quickly debussed and deployed for action (some of the supporting artillery actually opened fire). But Colonel Matthews' reconnaissance very soon disclosed that some 30 or 40 tanks now blocked the route, and realizing that the only hope of escape lay in avoidance, he decided to lead the battalion into the desert to the south and then turn east in a flanking movement which he hoped would by-pass the menacing German armour before first light.

D Company, under Captain R. E. C. Price, had with the Carrier Platoon been given permission to make their own way along the line of the coast. Without dispatch riders or adequate communications it was difficult to contact all the other vehicles; but the majority turned off the track to follow the Commanding Officer. (These included some Garwhal Rifles and a troop of Kent Yeomanry guns.)

As the day dawned several enemy tanks appeared on the left flank but at first did not open fire. Then, nearing the Trigh Capuzzo, the Germans opened up from armoured formations on three sides of the column; the convoy was forced to disperse and in the dust and confusion there was nothing for it but to attempt to run the gauntlet. Colonel Matthews held his party together and for seven hours they succeeded in driving behind the German forward troops before making their escape. Others made equally daring and audacious bids for freedom, but their total reached only 4 officers and about 100 soldiers, the remainder of the battalion, exceeding 500 all ranks, went into captivity.

A few days later Tobruk fell and Sollum became the most advanced British base in the Western Desert. The remnants of the battalion picked up their first-line reinforcements and took over a sector of the thinly-manned rearguard to the regrouping Eighth Army. (It was during this period that Major-General Rees, the commander on the spot, was heard to splutter into the microphone of his battle-caravan telephone, 'What are you asking me to do, defeat the M.C.C. with a scratch village cricket team?')

Several days later after an arduous and hazardous withdrawal through Mersa Matruh, the remnants of the battalion, still intact, arrived at the Canal Zone where they picked up a U.K. draft and travelled to Cyprus to join the 4th Indian Division.

Soon they re-organized into a mobile striking force, needing only a large draft of reinforcements to become once more fit for operations. Then, about mid-August, with a sense of real shock the battalion was ordered to disband. Most of the officers and men were transferred to the 1st King's Own but, in the interests of continuity, a small cadre sailed for home, where it was 'grafted' to the junior battalion of the Regiment, the 4th Monmouths, which lost its own identity to preserve and revitalize the old 1/24th.

During the severe winter of 1939/40 the 2nd Battalion moved from Londonderry to Barnard Castle where they trained in sub-arctic conditions on the northern moors. This rigorous training was to stand them in good stead when, on 10th April, 1940, they sailed with 24th Guards Brigade for Narvik, in Northern Norway, with the intention of capturing this tactically important iron-ore port and denying its facilities to the Germans.

They were based at Harstad in the Lofoten Islands but soon moved by stages to the Ankenes Peninsula just south of Narvik where, on 28th April, they took up defensive positions over an area of snow-clad mountain tops which stretched for five miles along the fiord. The conditions were grim. The French Chasseurs Alpins, ski-trained mountain troops with whom the battalion worked, found it difficult to operate in the deep snow while the British troops, without skis or snowshoes, were all but immobilized.

Apart from one incident when a German ski patrol stumbled by accident on Battalion Headquarters things remained fairly quiet until the afternoon of the 30th April when a platoon of D Company came under heavy mortar and shell fire which caused it to withdraw, three men being wounded in the process. This was followed up on the night of the 1st/2nd May by a dawn attack on what the enemy obviously thought to be a weak defensive position, because they used no artillery support. The attack began at about 0300 hours when the light allowed visibility at about 100 to 200 yards (the Midnight Sun was not due to rise for some two weeks, but it was never wholly dark) spearheaded by white-clad ski-troops firing tracer ammunition which showed up menacingly against the majestic snow-clad background. Fortunately their aim was inaccurate and D Company Commander (Captain C. F. Cox) concentrated his fire on the main enemy force along the track on his left flank.

An interesting inter-service development now took place when a British destroyer, attracted by the sound of battle, rounded Emmenes Point and took up a position a few yards off shore in full view of the Germans. Her Commander made a signal asking if all 24th patrols were in, and having received 'Yes' as an answer 'opened up with everything she possessed' at the attacking force. The frontal defensive fire from D Company and the heavy and demoralizing bombardment from the destroyer caused the enemy to break and run; then D Company made a sally to bring back seven prisoners, pausing to bury some of the German dead and capture a mass of enemy equipment.

D Company's losses were light, 3 killed and 3 wounded, but there were more casualties at Battalion Headquarters the next morning when a single German aircraft dropped a stick of bombs plumb across their position. On 5th May orders came to hand over to the Poles and move back to Harstad. Part of the 1st Scots Guards, who with the

1st Irish Guards were brigaded with the 2/24th, had already gone south to Mo, on the West Fiord, where with their Norwegian allies, they were facing the menace of a strong German army advancing from Southern Norway.

The Irish Guards embarked in a Polish ship which was attacked from the air and set on fire. They arrived back at Harstad minus their equipment (and many of their officers and men) and in the early hours of the 17th May the 2nd Battalion sailed for the West Fiord in the cruiser *Effingham*. The ship made all speed in the now-perpetual daylight until, at about 1950 hours, she struck a rock at 23 knots and immediately began to sink. There was no sign of panic as the troops assembled at their action stations to be taken off, without a single casualty, by an escorting destroyer.

When the battalion arrived back at Harstad they found that most of the reserve supplies had been issued to re-equip the Irish Guards; nevertheless two companies were kitted up and left for Bodo by destroyer that night. Within two days the remainder of the battalion followed to take up the defence of Bodo, on which the main German force was converging, forcing the Scots and Irish Guards (and the Independent Companies fighting with them) to withdraw. British air cover was confined to three aircraft, and soon the enemy were able to systematically bomb Bodo out of existence, leaving the defending force in a very precarious position.

By this time the disastrous events in France had forced the Allied Governments to order the evacuation of Norway and the 2nd Battalion, depressed but not defeated, returned to Clydeside, via the Orkney Islands, to refit and re-organize. This short but disastrous campaign cost the 2nd Battalion six dead and thirteen wounded, the first of many casualties in the Second World War. The battalion then left Scotland to return to Ulster, where they remained until December, 1941.

The next three years were spent in various parts of England in formations ranging from the 3rd Division to the 9th Armoured Division, where for a while they were downgraded in the scale of priority to the role of a draft-finding unit and found themselves lifting potatoes in East Anglia, which 'useful but homely task' they abandoned for a job more to their liking: training and preparation for 'Operation Overlord', the invasion of North West Europe, in a new formation called 56 Independent Brigade whose sign, appropriately, was a Sphinx (each of the battalions in it, 2nd Gloucester, 2nd Essex and 2/24th carried the Sphinx in its cap badge).

And so, on the historic 6th of June 1944, the 2/24th was the only Welsh battalion to land on the beaches of Nor-

Imperial War Museum

Men of the South Wales Borderers advance over open country in Holland on the way to Klundert.

mandy. Led by their C.O. Lieutenant-Colonel R. W. Craddock (who was to be wounded two days later) they waded ashore at Hable de Heurtot near Arromanches on the first stage of a journey which was to take them through France, Belgium and Holland and on into Germany, where they finished the war at Hamburg.

Their battles along that difficult, often blood-stained, journey are reflected in the battle-honours awarded to the Regiment: Normandy Landing, Sully, and Caen; the Risle Crossing, Le Havre; on to Arnhem and into Germany itself. These are some of the famous names which Major J. T. Boon, who served with the 2nd Battalion throughout the campaign, brings to life in his first-hand and first-rate History (published in 1955). In it can be found the names of those who suffered and survived and of the 164 who died between the Normandy coast and Hamburg to add to the glory of the 24th Regiment.

A further 584 officers and men were wounded, while 158 were posted 'missing', most of these casualties taking place in the heavy fighting of the first six months, in the period when Lieutenant-Colonel F. F. S. Barlow commanded the battalion. Figures can never convey either heartbreak or heroism but, for the record, the 2nd Battalion gained 46 decorations for gallantry, while 23 officers and men were mentioned in dispatches and a further 39 awarded certificates from either the Commander-in-Chief or the Brigade Commander. The closing words of Major Boon's History make a fitting end to their heroic endeavours:

> 'What can be said of the 2/24th's part in this epic? Amongst so many brave regiments serving is so many fine divisions in 21 Army Group it would be foolish to make too boastful claims, but it can truthfully be said that throughout the campaign the 2/24th lived up to its reputation as a first-class battalion of the Line, and there is not much higher praise that that.'

135

Men of the 24th move up through a swampy jungle road under snipers' fire.

The first of the new battalions of the Regiment raised in the early months of the war was the 5th Battalion, formed from older or medically-downgraded men, and destined for Home Service. They were disbanded early in 1943 when the danger of invasion had subsided.

The 6th Battalion was the only one to serve in the Far East, where they were a most notable representative, adding 'Burma 1944–45', 'North Arakan', 'Mayu Tunnels', 'Pinwe', 'The Shweli' and 'Myitson' to the battle-honours of the Regiment (three of these are carried on the Colours). Raised in July 1940 as an infantry battalion they sailed for India in 1942 and trained as a tank regiment, were reconverted into infantry, and fought with distinction in the Burma campaign. After the war they served in the East Indies before being disbanded in March 1946.

In a foreword to their History (published in 1956) Lieutenant-General (now Field-Marshal) Sir Francis Festing had this to say:

'. . . This Battalion served under me throughout the period that the 36th Division was fighting against the Japanese in various parts of Burma. Throughout that time their achievements were distinguished and I have no hesitation whatsoever in saying that they were quite one of the most virile of units that I have ever had under my command and I shall always remember them with affection and gratitude. They took part in nearly all the toughest fighting that our Division experienced and their achievements were all splendid. . . .'

The 7th Battalion was raised as infantry at about the same time as the 6th, but was soon converted to anti-aircraft artillery and fought in that role in North Africa and Italy.

Both the 2nd and 3rd Battalions of the Monmouthshire Regiment fought with distinction in North West Europe from shortly after D-Day until the end of the war. Their Histories form part of the series published between 1953 and 1956 and they give a fully documented account of their exploits throughout the campaign and beyond.

The 3rd Monmouthshires had the additional distinction of providing the 24th Regiment's twenty-third Victoria Cross, the only one to be awarded to the Corps of the South Wales Borderers during the War of 1939–1945. It was won by Corporal E. T. Chapman, in the Teutoburgerwald when, armed with a bren gun, 'he single-handedly halted or defeated repeated German attacks on his section and inflicted many casualties on the enemy. Under heavy fire he tried to carry his mortally wounded company commander fifty yards to safety. He continued fighting in spite of his own wounds. His action, by gaining much needed time, enabled the force to be re-organized on the ridge.'

This supreme act of courage, in what was virtually the last action of the 3rd Monmouthshires in the campaign, is a fitting note on which to bring to an end this short account of the Regiment's contribution to the war of 1939–1945.

General Morgan-Owen had retired at his own request from the Colonelcy in May 1944 so that Major-General D. G. Johnson, V.C., C.B., D.S.O., M.C., could become Colonel of the Regiment, and it was under the latter's leadership that the 24th faced the coming of peace.

CHAPTER THIRTEEN

1946–1968

I N T H E W A K E of the war came the inevitable changes in the military establishment. The rapid run-down of the forces produced problems to which, although they had been well-studied, there were no clear-cut answers. The Cardwell system had worked well in its time but it was now over-due for replacement. As early as 1943 there had been strong advocates of a Corps of Infantry, whose argument was that as Artillery and other arms were organized on a corps basis, making recruitment and reinforcement a comparatively easy matter, why not the Infantry?

Field-Marshal Montgomery, as usual, had forthright views on this subject: 'We must be very careful what we do with the British Infantry. They are the people who do the hard fighting and the killing. If we mess them about we may well lose the war. Their fighting spirit is based largely on morale and regimental *esprit de corps*. On no account must anyone tamper with this.' So the Corps of Infantry planners were quietened and it now seemed that some kind of grouping based on either a territorial or traditional basis must evolve. The Light Infantry had a common tradition (going back to the Peninsula) on which to base a group; so, because of race, did the 'tribal' regiments of Scotland, Wales and Northern Ireland. It was natural in these circumstances that the Royal Welch Fusiliers, the South Wales Borderers and the Welch Regiment should form the Welsh Group (renamed in 1947 The Welsh Brigade) to foster 'the development of a healthy *esprit de corps* based on nationality'.

While this was happening the two Regular battalions were readjusting themselves to the rigours of 'peace'-time soldiering. For the 2nd Battalion the road was a short one for on 31st May 1948 they were formally disbanded, the soldiers having been posted to other battalions within the Welsh Brigade. In the same year the Regiment received the Freedom of the ancient Borough of Brecon (having been granted the Freedom of Newport, Monmouthshire, in 1947).

The 1st Battalion, now commanded by Lieutenant-Colonel C. F. Cox, sailed from Southampton for Palestine on the 11th October, 1945, but after a short stay of some seven months moved across to the island of Cyprus to take on the thankless task of guarding the thousands of Jews who had been intercepted and detained while trying to illegally enter the 'Promised Land'. When, in 1949, the British Government laid down the Palestine Mandate the battalion went to the Sudan where C and D Companies were sent on detachment to Gebeit, in the Red Sea hills, while the rest of the unit stayed at Khartoum.

They were scarcely a week in their new station when a Tactical Headquarters and one company (B) were sent up to Asmara, in the former Italian Colony of Eritrea, to assist the 1st Royal Berkshires in keeping the peace amongst the Copts, Moslems and backward pagans who inhabited this vast, largely desert, territory. Superimposed on the native peoples was a kind of 'top layer' of Italians of the managerial and artisan classes, many of them Eritrean born and all of them cordially hated by the natives. This situation had produced a militant quasi-political element called Shifta (a local word for bandit) who had partly abandoned their cattle-raiding and general thuggery for the more fashionable occupation of killing Italians and looting their property.

Companies of the 1st Battalion, on a rota basis, now took

the opportunity of operating against the Shifta, finding the high plateau around Asmara a pleasant change from the heat of Khartoum. Early in 1950 the battalion concentrated in Eritrea, co-operating with the Royal Berkshires, the Eritrean Police and a local ancillary native force called the 'Banda', against the Shifta. These activities, while not eliminating the bandits, were extremely valuable in training young soldiers and junior officers.

Meanwhile the Colonelcy had changed hands when, on the last day of 1949, Major-General D. G. Johnson, V.C., C.B., D.S.O., M.C., retired and General Sir A. Reade Godwin-Austen, K.C.S.I., C.B., O.B.E., M.C., a distinguished officer of the 24th, who had been Principal Administrative Officer in India, became Colonel of the Regiment. Almost two years later, when Eritrea was formally united with Ethiopia, the 1st Battalion left Asmara, and returned for a short spell to Wales. There they stayed at Sennybridge Camp, exercising their right to march through the streets of the towns of Brecon and Newport with 'bayonets fixed, drums beating and Colours flying'.

In January 1953 they moved to Germany where, in mid-tour, they were suddenly alerted for a trip to the Canal Zone which, to the relief of many, was cancelled after the advance party had actually started to move. But the next posting was a more exciting one, for in September 1955 they sailed from Southampton for active service against the Communist Terrorists in the guerilla war then raging in the Malayan Peninsula.

The Regiment landed in Singapore on 19th October, and after a few weeks training at Kota Tinggi took over their operational area from the 1st East Yorkshires, who were due to return to U.K. The camp was on the edge of the primitive airfield of Kluang, a small polyglot community in mid-Johore where Battalion Headquarters was established in a dilapidated building (once occupied by the

Japanese) and most of the companies detached in operational camps. The so-called 'Emergency' was then in its eighth year and had entered the third phase, which consisted of isolating the scattered pockets of C.T. (as the Communist Terrorists were universally called); preventing movement between them; starving them out and, acting often on the invaluable information provided by the Special Branch Police, ambushing and killing them.

The Welsh soldiers of the 1st Battalion took to the jungle like a duck takes to water. Within a few months an important local C.T. leader named Kok Fui, a murderer and extortioner who had evaded capture for many years, had been killed by a National Service Second Lieutenant. After this early start they went on from strength to strength, moving in 1956 to Segamat, 60 miles farther north in the State of Johore, where their crowning achievement was the destruction of the notorious Selumpur Branch of the C.T., culminating in the surrender of its infamous leader, Ming Lee.

To assess the great achievements of the 1st Battalion in Malaya one must read the book *Shoot to Kill* by Richard Miers.*

Between July 1957 and April 1958 the battalion was engaged on Internal Security duties in Singapore, but kept two companies on rotation in anti-terrorist operations at the southern tip of Johore. They came home at the end of April 1958 and went to Dering Lines, in Brecon, where they became part of 2 Infantry Brigade in the recently formed Strategic Reserve.

During their absence in the Far East sweeping changes had been made in the Armed Forces. Many famous regiments had lost their identity and widespread amalgamations had caused redundancy among both officers and men. The Welsh Brigade were fortunate in escaping this

---

* The late Brigadier R. C. H. Miers, D.S.O. and Bar, O.B.E., published by Faber in 1959.

'axe' but, like the other Brigades, later lost their traditional Regimental Depots and concentrated their sole training establishment at Cwrt-y-Gollen, not far from Crickhowell, just inside the Breconshire border. A single cap badge consisting of the 'upright' plumes of the Prince of Wales's crest, with its Motto 'Ich Dien', was adopted for the whole Brigade and other changes in dress and embellishments were gradually introduced. The appointment of a Brigade Colonel came into being so that the organization of the three regiments could be better co-ordinated, while the actual Brigade Depot was commanded in turn by Lieutenant-Colonels drawn from different battalions of the Welsh Brigade.

A Regimental Headquarters, small but effective, was retained at the old traditional Depot towns and each regiment still kept its own Colonel. General Godwin-Austen had retired in 1954 and on 18th April of that year Major-General F. R. G. Matthews, C.B., D.S.O., who had commanded the 1st Battalion in the desert in 1942, became the new Colonel of the 24th. Under his guidance the 1st Battalion received new Colours at Ebbw Vale on 25th July, 1958 (in a joint ceremony shared by the 2nd Monmouthshires). The Queen was represented at the presentation by H.R.H. the Duke of Edinburgh and shortly afterwards the old Colours were laid up with their illustrious predecessors in the Regimental Chapel at Brecon Cathedral.

In late summer 1959, under the Command of Lieutenant-Colonel P. J. Martin, the battalion moved to Germany for a three-year tour as part of 11 Infantry Brigade Group, based on Minden. During this time General Matthews relinquished the Colonelcy and was succeeded on 1st January 1962 by Major-General David Peel Yates, D.S.O., O.B.E., who had commanded the 1st Battalion in Brunswick from 1953 to 1955.

Lt.-General Sir David Peel-Yates, K.C.B., C.V.O., D.S.O., O.B.E., Colonel of the South Wales Borderers December 31st, 1961

Towards the end of 1963, as the weather worsened, the 1st Battalion flew 'in penny packets' to Hong Kong, the last plane-load touching down at Kai Tak on Friday, 29th November. Almost immediately they commenced training for their Internal Security role and under their Commanding Officer, Lieutenant-Colonel A. R. Evill, reconnoitred the rocky foothills of the New Territories on the borders of Communist China.

One of their more unusual assignments was the provision of a party of one officer and fifteen soldiers to form part of the United Nations Platoon which formed the Honour Guards at Seoul, in South Korea. Their American hosts (they were attached to the 8th United States Honor Guard Company) could never quite get used to the Welsh custom of designating a soldier by his last two numbers only and gaped in wonder as the troops answered their names on parade:

'Evans 45.'
'Sir!'
'63?'
'Sir!'
'79?'
'Sir!'
'Jones 01.'
'Sir!'
'77?'
'Sir!' and so on through the Morgans' and Williams'. They eventually got used to the 'Welsh babies' as they nicknamed the small-statured 24th, saying: 'You've got a real good bunch of guys there.'

At sport the battalion really excelled, winning the Land Forces Boxing Team Championship and carrying off the Far East Rugby Cup, while at sailing they literally swept the board. The one main disappointment was that recruiting for the battalion was not good enough to bring it up to the required strength for active service against the Indonesians in Borneo. This was partly overcome by sending down individual platoons for attachment to battalions like the Scots Guards and the Durham Light Infantry, and this gave a taste of valuable battle experience to several young officers and N.C.O.s. A composite platoon was made up from the battalion to go down to Okinawa island, in the South Pacific, to train with the United States Marines.

It was a rather sad battalion which arrived back at Lydd, in Kent, in midsummer, 1966. The Commanding Officer, Lieutenant-Colonel J. N. Somerville, knowing that there were few areas around Folkestone to rival 'Susy Wong's' Wan Chai, must have been pondering on how to occupy the off-duty time of his exuberant soldiers when the news came that the battalion was to be posted to Swaziland in early 1967.

Then Swaziland was granted independence and in

January 1967 the battalion, leaving their families behind at Lydd, started a nine-month tour in troubled Aden with the additional duty of maintaining a Company Detachment in Botswana. They moved into the terrorist-infested district of Ma'alla and soon made their presence felt, as this extract from the Commander-in-Chief's Commendation awarded to one of the battalion's young N.C.O.s shows:

'This action took place at 13.50 hours on 11th February, 1967, at a time when a curfew was in force in Aden to prevent violence and hostile demonstrations. Lance-Corporal Jones was N.C.O. in charge of a party consisting of himself, a driver, two escorts and a 3-ton vehicle. They were returning to their Company position after delivering a number of curfew breakers to Ma'alla Police Station.

'As they were driving south down Admiralty Road a hostile crowd of about one hundred local nationals, carrying banners, suddenly entered the road in front of them from the area of some houses to the west of Admiralty Road. The 3-ton vehicle was brought to a stop about thirty yards from the crowd which then began advancing towards it in a hostile manner. With only four men and a large vulnerable vehicle, Lance-Corporal Jones was faced with an ugly situation requiring initiative and quick action. He took control and, having called on the crowd to halt with no result, he ordered fire to be opened. A total of eight rounds were fired and four of the crowd were hit. This action caused the crowd to disperse rapidly to their homes.

'By his prompt and immediate action in an extremely dangerous situation this young N.C.O. gained the initiative and prevented the situation from getting out of hand. His action had the subsequent effect of deterring any further demonstrations in the "C" Class area of Ma'alla.'

While the Regiment were helping to maintain the *status quo* in Aden Mr. Wilson's Government were busily altering the shape of the Defence Forces, and in a White Paper issued in July, 1967, sweeping reforms were introduced which imposed drastic cuts. The Infantry are to be reduced by eight battalions and their organization altered to six 'Divisions' tailored to absorb the existing Brigades. One of these Divisions is to be called the Prince of Wales', and in it the Welsh Brigade, reduced by one battalion, is to take its place with the Mercian and Wessex Brigades.

The loss of the one Welsh battalion was dealt with in the White Paper in these words:

'Welsh Brigade.

'The Brigade will reduce by one battalion which is to be the 1st Battalion The Welch Regiment. On the recommendation of the Council of Colonels, The Welch Brigade will amalgamate with The South Wales Borderers to form a new Regiment.'

This edict thus paved the way for the return to the 24th of the descendants of one of its 2nd Battalions, which in April 1758 left it to become the 69th (later, with the 41st, becoming The Welch Regiment). But the form and content of the 'new Regiment', its name (even its regimental home) remains to be hammered out by the planners; while from the Shades old 24th men like Dering and Marlborough and a myriad ghostly 'rank and file' silently contemplate the possible interruption of 279 years of continuous unbroken service to the Crown.

By the 20th of September, 1967, the 1st Battalion was clear of Aden, its operational duties having been taken on by 45 Royal Marine Commando on the 8th of that month. What had they achieved in their nine-month tour? The cold statistics, even, are revealing. The battalion was engaged in some 300 terrorist attacks involving 80 by machine-gun or automatic small arms fire; 191 grenade attacks; 8 attacks by mortars and 21 by rocket. Twelve

A watchful Lance-Corporal on guard in Aden

other attacks by mines and explosives make up the balance.

Their Special Branch Squad carried out over 40 specially directed raids to uncover many caches of arms and ammunition, three of them being of major importance. They recovered Blindicide rockets and their launchers; sub-machine-guns and pistols; 'Jumping Jack' and anti-tank mines and many assorted grenades, detonators and fuses, all of which could have dealt injury or death to the British in Aden.

They killed 11 terrorists, wounded 11 and captured 18. The price they paid was the death of two of their soldiers (Private John Barry and Private Melville Jones) and the wounding of 33 others. But behind the statistics lies a story of stoic endurance and steady, soldierly action in the face of well-planned, but sometimes frantic (even fanatical) provocation.

In the words of their Commanding Officer, Lieutenant-Colonel J. N. Somerville, 'We very soon established a domination over the area (Ma'alla), and a reputation for ourselves which included the important elements of fear and respect.'

With the help of the ever-present Sappers they walled up all entrances from the south into their 'beat', thus cutting down the number of grenade attacks in the shopping area, for one of their main tasks was to guard the 4,000 British Servicemen, wives and children who comprised the 1,700 families living in the large blocks of flats around the street called 'Murder Mile' in Ma'alla main.

Although widely dispersed (their Headquarters were in Falaise Camp, in Little Aden, some twenty-four miles away) they were responsible for 'law and order' in Ma'alla, and this, as most soldiers know, means everything from Internal Security, though static guards, to nursemaid duties for absent mothers.

As early as the 16th of January, only a few days after the arrival of the main body, a complicated radio network linked the Commanding Officer to his detached companies, providing an effective means of communication which extended some 4,000 miles to Botswana in South Africa, where one company, regularly rotated, was on detached duty. This detached company stationed in Francistown, once the main city of Bechuana, was responsible for the protection of the Central African Relay Station, which broadcasts B.B.C. programmes to the adjacent African territories. It provided almost the only relief from the rigours of Aden. B Company (Rorke's Drift Company) were the first to go, followed by the other two rifle companies. All three of them made the most of the many opportunities to get away on safari and, naturally, to get down to Isandhlwana and to Rorke's Drift, where they were most enthusiastically received by the South African people.

One of the posters displayed by FLOSY in Aden.

The last company was withdrawn from Francistown on the 16th of August in time to join the phasing-out programme which finally reunited the battalion with their eagerly waiting families in Lydd on the Kentish Coast. There, after a well-earned leave, they will re-train and re-organize, waiting, as they have for more than two and three-quarter centuries, for the call to action.

No one knows what the future holds: this cliché must now be uppermost in the minds of those who have the welfare of the Regiment at heart. Perhaps the words of the Colonel of the Regiment in his Notes in the current issue of the Regimental Journal can help to put things in their proper perspective: '. . . Whatever our inner feelings the news of the cuts (the amalgamations) puts an end to a long period of speculation and uncertainty which has done the Army no good. We have now got to make a new regiment for Wales, composed of the Twenty-Fourth and the Welch Regiment, and that will require the maximum amount of goodwill from everyone connected with the

150

two Regiments and especially from the ex-members. . . .'

And there we must leave it, for forces are at work, both economic and political, which may well lead to further cuts in the Armed Services. We can only pray that, through it all, the identity of the old 24th Foot will be preserved.

THE REGIMENTAL MARCH OF THE SOUTH WALES BORDERERS

Men of Harlech.

(Rhyfelgyrch gwyr Harlech.)

The South Wales Borderers

1689-1968

1689	Regiment founded as Dering's Regiment.
1689–91	Service in Ireland.
1692–97	War with France.
1702	John Churchill, Duke of Marlborough, Colonel of the Regiment.
1702–12	War of the Spanish Succession—Blenheim, Ramillies, Oudenarde, Malplaquet.
1713–40	Spent on station in Ireland, apart from the Vigo Expedition in 1719.
1741	'War of Jenkins' Ear'—Cartagena.
1742–51	Home Station.
1752–56	Minorca.
1757	2nd Battalion formed (later to become the 69th Foot, and then the 2nd Welch Regiment).
1760–63	Operations on the Continent against the French.
1764–74	Gibraltar. Home station.
1775–81	American War of Independence.
1784–1800	Home station. Canada.
1801–02	Egypt.

	1st Battalion		*2nd Battalion*
1805–10	South Africa—Cape of Good Hope.	1804	Raised at Warwick.
		1809–14	Peninsular War—Talavera, Busaco, Fuentes d'Onor, Salamanca,

1805–1810 *cont.*			Vittoria, Pyrenees, Nivelle, Orthes.
1811–19	India.	1814	Disbanded.
–46	Home station. Canada.	1858	Raised again at Sheffield.
1846–61	India. Second Sikh War.	1860	Mauritius.
1862–71	Home station. Malta, Gibraltar.	1865–73	Burma. Andaman Islands. India.
1872	South Africa.	1874–76	Home station.
1877–78	Kaffir War.	1877–78	Kaffir War.
1879	Zulu War.	1879	Zulu War— Rorke's Drift.
1880–92	Home station.	1880–82	Gibraltar.
		1882–88	India. Burma.
1892–95	Egypt.	1892	Aden.
1895–97	Gibraltar.	1893–1900	Home Station.
1897–1910	India.	1900–04	South Africa— South African War.
		1904–10	Home station.
1910–14	Home station.	1910–12	South Africa.
		1912–14	China.

1914–18   The Great War.
Fourteen battalions in all, which saw service in France, Gallipoli, Egypt, Mesopotamia and Macedonia.

1st Battalion		*2nd Battalion*	
1919–28	Home station.	1919–27	India.
1928–41	Egypt. Palestine. Hong Kong. India.	1927–29	Aden.
		1929–35	Home station.
		1935–36	Malta. Palestine.
		1936–39	Home station.

1939-45	The Second World War.
	1st Battalion—Iraq. Desert. Cyprus.
	2nd Battalion—Norway. Normandy.
	6th Battalion—Far East.
	7th Battalion—North Africa. Italy.
1945–51	Palestine. Cyprus. Sudan
1948	2nd Battalion disbanded.
1951–52	Home station.
1953–58	Germany. Malaya.
1958–59	Home station.
1959–67	Germany. Hong Kong. Aden.
September 1967	Home station.